**The Four-Blocks®
Literacy Model**

# Shared Reading with Big Books
### Lessons Using Building-Blocks™ and Four-Blocks® Strategies

## by
## Dorothy P. Hall
## and
## Joseph M. Fuhrmann

## Carson-Dellosa Publishing Co., Inc.
## Greensboro, NC

## Dedications

To my editor, Joey Bland, and all my Four-Blocks friends who constantly support me in my work.

This book, and so many others, become a reality because of the hard work of the people at Carson-Dellosa Publishing Company, especially Joey Bland, Four-Blocks editor! Joey always goes the extra mile to see that Pat and I are satisfied with Four-Blocks books. Thanks, Joey!

Dottie Hall

To Kathy, who said I could and should write long before I ever did. Thanks for your encouragement, support, and love.

Joe Fuhrmann

## Credits

**Editor:**
Joey Bland

**Cover Design:**
Annette Hollister-Papp

**Cover Photo:**
Taken at Westchester Academy in High Point, North Carolina

**Layout Design:**
Jon Nawrocik

© 2002, Carson-Dellosa Publishing Company, Inc., Greensboro, North Carolina 27425. Four-Blocks and associated logos are registered trademarks of Carson-Dellosa Publishing Co., Inc. The purchase of this material entitles the buyer to reproduce activities for classroom use only—not for commercial resale. Reproduction of these materials for an entire school or district is prohibited. No part of this book may be reproduced (except as noted above), stored in a retrieval system, or transmitted in any form or by any means (mechanically, electronically, recording, etc.) without the prior written consent of Carson-Dellosa Publishing Co., Inc.

Printed in the USA • All rights reserved

ISBN 0-88724-868-3

# Table of Contents

## Lessons

## Table of Contents

# Foreword

It has been over ten years since Pat Cunningham and I started the Four-Blocks® Literacy Model (Cunningham, Hall, and Defee, 1991, 1998; Cunningham, Hall, and Sigmon, 1998) in one first-grade classroom in North Carolina. Four Blocks is not a curriculum—it does not tell teachers what to teach. Four Blocks is a framework to put your curriculum in. Four Blocks tells teachers how to teach the things they teach. We have watched Four Blocks grow as wonderful teachers in this country and in other countries have embraced the practices. Kindergarten teachers have adopted Building Blocks™ (Cunningham and Hall, 1997; Hall and Williams, 2000), our kindergarten program, as quickly as first- and second-grade teachers have adopted Four Blocks. As we got to know Four-Blocks teachers on the World Wide Web and at workshops, we were amazed at their knowledge and dedication. We realized that the best teachers were using Four Blocks in their classrooms and helping others to learn the model. Now, we know why Four Bocks was spreading so fast!

One of the teachers who was "spreading the word" on Four Blocks is Joe Fuhrmann from Kankakee, Illinois. He told his "story" in *True Stories from Four-Blocks® Classrooms* (Cunningham and Hall, 2001). It was then that Pat and I learned Joe could also write. When Pat, Jim, and I wrote *Guided Reading the Four-Blocks® Way* (Cunningham, Hall, and Cunningham, 2000), we told teachers how we would use a variety of materials to teach the reading skills and strategies young children need to learn. It was then that Joe looked at all the wonderful big books on the market and realized that many teachers wanted to know how to use them "the Four-Blocks way." This book is the result of Joe's Four-Blocks expertise and hard work. Thanks, Joe, for helping Building-Blocks and Four-Blocks teachers have one more tool for their teaching!

*Dorothy P. Hall*

# Shared Reading with Big Books

## Introduction

Shared reading with big books is a wonderful way to expose emergent readers to books and print. Big books can also be used to teach beginning reading skills and strategies. The purpose of big books is to share the lap experience with a class. When a child sits on his mother's (or caregiver's) lap, the child sees both the pictures and the print. Children, who have been read to from an early age know a lot about stories, books, and print from these reading experiences. This knowledge comes from observation. These young children see books up close—looking not only at the pictures as the story is read to them, but also looking at the print. They notice how the reader turns pages and that when there is a lot of reading, there are a lot of marks on the page. These children soon find out these marks are letters, and they are grouped together to make words, and these words make sentences. When parents talk about that "big word" or "long sentence," children learn the jargon of school. Children who have had these book experiences before they begin their formal schooling profit from our instruction. Children who have not had these experiences need to have them in school. Shared reading of big books can provide these experiences for those children who have not been so fortunate at home. What the teacher says and does before and after the reading can move all children forward in their literacy learning.

There are many wonderful big books on the market today. Some are years old, and others are "hot off the press." The original big books used in grade one were the first of the three preprimers in some basal reading programs. Some schools just bought the small versions for students and other schools bought the big book and the smaller versions, too. The stories were about a "typical," middle-class, white, American family. Using a big book allowed children to watch the teacher open the book, turn the pages, see the pictures, and "track print" (if they pointed to the words on each page). The big book made it easier for the teacher to make sure every child was on the right page and following along. The teacher could also "show" children the words they wanted to talk about and the letters they wanted the children to notice at the beginning of words.

The next big books used in schools were "literature-based" and were the result of the "whole-language" movement of the 1980s. The publishers chose appropriate stories for kindergarten, first, and second grades, and published them in big book form to "share" with the class. Often they published little books just like the big book for children to read by themselves. Big books and shared reading became the rage and schools and teachers purchased them for kindergarten, first, and second grades, whether they used a basal reading series or not. Publishers responded by putting out a lot of big books—some appropriate and some not. Some big books had too much text, and teachers could not "track print" and point to words. The difficulty of the words, size of the print, and the amount of text in these books made it impossible to use them for shared reading, so the teachers just read the books to the whole class.

The "phonics-first" movement in the 1990s led publishers to concentrate more on phonics workbooks and phonics readers. Guided Reading, as described by Fountas and Pinnel (1996), called for little books and little groups, and the big books took a back seat in their instructional methods. Fountas and Pinnel called for "Guided Reading" using small group instruction that focused on word identification. Teachers were to teach children how to use the three cuing systems—but their book did not focus on comprehension. Soon critics were asking, "Where's the comprehension instruction?" and many teachers were asking, "How can I do all these little groups when most of my children can't work independently?" This problem was most evident among children whose background experiences did not prepare them to work "independently" while the teacher worked with a group.

The call for a "balanced reading program" led teachers back to big books with which they could teach skills and strategies to young children in a whole class format. The teachers could then offer children a double dose of reading and have them read little books and good literature "on their own level" at a self-selected (independent) reading time. Both Building Blocks and Four Blocks are balanced reading programs.

During the last year or two, a number of school publishers have brought out many more wonderful big books. Teachers are realizing that they can work with a whole class of students and still teach to the many levels within the class. Teachers can "do it all" in one lesson if they have different expectations for the many children in their classrooms.

## How Shared Reading Is a Multilevel Activity

Children come to school at different literacy levels. They also learn in different ways. Shared reading of big books provides children who already know something about reading and know some words an opportunity to concentrate on the words and learn more about them. By observing the pictures and print and with coaching from the teacher about the three cuing systems, these children begin to notice similarities and differences in words and learn even more about how words work. As the teacher talks about what is happening in these books and makes connections to things the children already know, the children learn how to gain meaning from print. They learn how to think about what the author is writing about. They learn more about stories and how they are written from reading fiction. They learn information about different topics when reading nonfiction. These "above average" children are really reading these books even though they are written above grade level.

Children in kindergarten and first grade (in some schools these children are also found in second grade) who have had little or no experience with print, develop concepts about print as they see the teacher turning the page, reading from left to write, reading from top to bottom, and hear the teacher talking about the ending "marks" on each sentence. They learn how to use the pictures to gain more meaning. That is why picture books have pictures—much of the message is contained in the pictures! "What fun, what fun!" says the text, but looking at the picture is the only way to find out how the characters are having fun. "Oh, No!" What is wrong? Look at the picture and you find out what is happening. These emergent readers gain confidence with the knowledge that they are learning to read alongside their friends, not separated and told they are "not ready to read" yet. These children, who are not as far along in their literacy learning as many schools would like, are learning what they need during shared reading and doing it in a way that makes sense to them and doesn't hurt their self-esteem.

What about those "average" children—children that are not reading well but who know something about letters and sounds and a few "interesting-to-them" words? Children who are ready to begin learning some words, but who cannot really read these big books, learn some words and something about fiction and nonfiction. These students learn this as the teacher points out the letters and sounds they know in some of the new words that are repeated in these books. These children can take part in the group discussions after shared reading. Once the teacher reads the book, they easily pick up the pattern or learn to use the pictures to help them read words. Most importantly, all children develop the desire to learn to read and the confidence that they are all learning to read.

## Choosing a Big Book for Shared Reading

The best books for shared reading for the youngest readers are predictable by pictures or print. When big books are predictable by pictures, then children can almost "read the words" by looking at the pictures. When big books are predictable by print, the children hear the pattern and are soon joining in and "sharing the reading," thus the name "shared reading!"

---

**What to Look for When Choosing a Big Book for Shared Reading**

1.  The book must be very predictable, with repetitive sentences, pictures to support these sentences, and not too much print on each page.

2.  The book should be enjoyable and appealing to most of the children, since the entire class will work with the same big book.

3.  The book must be able to "take the students someplace" conceptually. Most teachers spend a week or two with a book—reading, rereading, acting out the story, and building connections to the themes or units to extend the children's knowledge.

    (Hall and Cunningham, 1997)

---

## A Shared Reading Lesson

With shared reading, as with any reading lesson, there is a before-reading stage, a during-reading stage, and an after-reading stage. In the before-reading part of the lesson, the teacher builds prior knowledge and gets ready to read by talking about experiences related to the book. The teacher talks about some of the new and/or important words in the book—words that the children need to know to be able to read and understand the book.

The during-reading part of the lesson should involve the teacher reading the big book more than once. Shared, choral, or echo reading may be part of this stage. The first time, the book is read to the class just for the enjoyment of listening to a good book. The second time the teacher reads the book, she may want the children to join in and share the reading of the book or be her echo and read after her. Pointing to the words as the teacher reads them helps children focus on both the repetition of sound and repetition of print. During subsequent readings, children will be asked to read again and do more and more of the reading.

In the after-reading part of the lesson, the teacher focuses on comprehension and understanding by leading a discussion and/or asking questions. If it is a "story," the teacher may ask *who, what, where, when,* or *why*. The teacher may also ask, How do you know that? The class might act out the story or draw pictures. Sometimes the teacher tosses a beach ball with story questions written on each stripe. After-reading is also the time to go from talking about the whole story to talking about words (long words, short words, rhyming words, high-frequency words, etc.). Finally, the teacher might talk about letters and sounds connected to some of the words in the book. She will focus on letter sounds that the students need to be aware of if they want to figure out some new words in another book.

## Planning Lessons for Shared Reading

Many big books on the market include lesson plans. The purpose of these lesson plans is to tie in with a theme or to teach a certain skill. There are even big books written for a certain grade level or more recently, a reading level. Some big books are just good stories that young children enjoy and their interest spans more than one grade level or age. Often the publishers of basal textbooks buy the rights to use a good story, make it into a big book, then try to please everyone and every state with a mandated curriculum when they write the lesson plans for the book. The teacher is then left trying to decide just what to do or how to get it all done! The truth is that you cannot and should not try to do everything in some of the teacher's manuals. You would never "get it all done" and if you did, your students wouldn't read enough.

If what we have learned from decades of research is true (you learn to read by reading, not by "doing" skills and strategies worksheets and workbooks), then we must read every day during "reading time." That just makes sense to us and many wonderful teachers across this country. If the goal of reading instruction is to be able to both decode text and comprehend or understand the text that has been read, then "Guided Reading" lessons must work on both of these skills. But the teacher's manuals often fail in planning reading into every lesson. *Shared Reading with Big Books* does not fail in that objective.

## Using This Book

This book includes lessons for 50 big books. Some of these big books are stories or "fiction," and some of the big books are informational books or "nonfiction." Each lesson contains a summary of the big book, a five-day lesson plan, a two-day lesson plan, and other books and activities to extend the big book. The five-day lesson plan is for teachers who want to use this big book over five days or a week. Most kindergarten teachers want to do this, as do first-grade teachers early in the year. The two-day plan is for teachers in first and second grades to use. Teachers in Four-Blocks classrooms use a two-day plan for the "easy" or "drop back" days. Teachers will have appropriate before-, during-, and after-reading activities for every day they use the book, regardless of whether they want to use it for two or five days. They will also have lessons that focus on decoding skills and comprehension skills. The lessons have different activities that will help teach to the many and varied reading levels of children in your class. Most of all, teachers and children will find these activities to be enjoyable, and reading should be an enjoyable experience for all children, regardless of their literacy level! We hope you enjoy these lesson plans as much as we enjoyed writing them for you.

## Four-Blocks Activities/Strategies

Two of the Four-Blocks Activities/Strategies used in this book are Beach Ball and Webs.

### Beach Ball

The Beach Ball is a real beach ball that has a question written in black, permanent marker on each colored stripe of the ball. Here are the some questions teachers use:

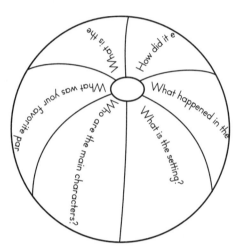

- What is the title and who is the author?
- Who are the main characters?
- What is the setting?
- What happened in the story?
- How did it end?
- What was your favorite part?

Another option is to use sentence starters such as:

- My favorite part was . . .
- The setting was . . .
- The main characters were . . .
- In the beginning . . .
- In the middle . . .
- At the end . . .

The class forms a large circle and the teacher begins by tossing the ball to a student. The teacher assists the student who catches the ball in reading one of the questions, then gives all the students opportunities to answer the question. This continues until all the questions have been thoroughly answered.

A pre-printed Beach Ball is available from Carson-Dellosa (see page 176).

### Webs

A web is a graphic organizer drawn on a piece of chart paper, a transparency, or on the board. To complete a web, the teacher writes the topic in the large center circle, and spokes lead from this center circle to smaller circles (subtopics). The teacher will add spokes to these smaller circles with the details from the big book.

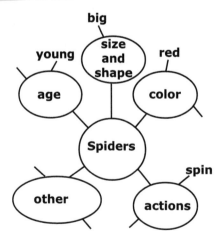

# A Pair of Socks

## Stuart J. Murphy
### (Scholastic Big Books, 1996)

A lonely sock thoroughly searches the laundry room for his missing match. Along the way, the sock encounters a variety of different colored and patterned socks.

**Purpose:**
Build background and read for enjoyment.

**Before:**
- Cover Talk—Ask, "What do you notice? What is the dog doing? Who is able to find the word **socks**? What about the word **pair**? What could happen in this story?"
- Picture Walk—Start a discussion of each page with the question, "What do you notice?" On each page, take notice of the item from the laundry room. Do not go past page 21 of the big book. Ask, "How do you think this story will end?"

**During:**
- Read Aloud—Read the book aloud to students.
- Shared Reading—Invite students to join in and share the reading.

**After:**
- Discussion—Ask, "Have you ever lost one of your socks? What happened? Where did you find it?"

---

**Purpose:**
Identify the beginning, middle, and end of the story.

**Preparation/Materials Needed:**
- Three sentence strips
- Pocket chart with cards labeled: **Beginning, Middle, End**
- Beach Ball

**Before:**
- Retelling—Let the children retell the story during a picture walk. Ask, "What happened at the beginning? In the middle? At the end? Let's read to find our if we're right."

**During:**
- Echo Reading—Read a line and let the children be your echo, repeating the line after you.

**After:**
- Discussion and Writing—Ask, "What happened at the beginning? In the middle? At the end?" Write students' responses on sentence strips and post them in the pocket chart.
- Beach Ball Questions—Toss the beach ball. Assist the student who catches the ball in reading one of the questions. Allow students to answer the question. Encourage them to refer to the pocket chart or book cover when giving their answers.

> **EXAMPLE**
>
> **Beginning**
> The red and blue striped sock cannot find its mate.
>
> **Middle**
> A dog picks up the sock and brings the sock to his basket.
>
> **End**
> The sock found its mate in the dog's basket.

## Purpose:
To reread the book and discuss these high-frequency words: **and, this, not.**
## Preparation/Materials Needed:
- Beach Ball with questions

**Before:**
- Retelling—Use the cover as a catalyst for retelling the story.

**During:**
- Choral Reading and Highlighting—The whole class reads the text with you or you can assign parts to be read by different children. Stop after each two-page spread. Allow students to find, highlight, and tally the words: **and, this,** and **not.**

**After:**
- Discussion—Talk about the number of times you found these high-frequency words, sometimes called "popcorn" words because they keep "popping" up in students' reading.

---

## Purpose:
Complete a cloze summary of the story.
## Preparation/Materials Needed:
- Chart paper with the cloze summary shown in the example (Note: The underlined words in the example should be left out, then filled in during the lesson.)

**Before:**
- Picture Walk—Do a picture walk. List all the places the sock looked for its missing mate.

**During:**
- Choral Reading—Assign groups and choral read in two parts, alternating the reading of two-page spreads.
- Finding and Writing—Find the two words used to describe each sock and write them on a self-stick note. Place the notes beside their locations on the list created in the Before step.

**After:**
- Completing the Cloze—Use the list from the Before and During steps to complete the summary.

> **EXAMPLE**
>
> The sock in the <u>laundry bag</u> was <u>stinky</u> and <u>grimy</u>.
>
> The sock in the <u>washer</u> was <u>sudsy</u> and <u>slimy</u>.
>
> The sock in the dryer was <u>warm</u> and <u>fluffy</u>.
>
> The sock in the <u>laundry basket</u> was <u>folded</u> and <u>puffy</u>.
>
> But, the sock in the <u>dog's basket</u> was a perfect match.

---

## Purpose:
Participate in Doing the Book or acting out the story.
## Preparation/Materials Needed:
- The "Props"—pictures of **socks** that match the ones in the book; large pictures of a **laundry bag, washer, dryer, laundry basket,** and **dog basket**

**Before:**
- Presenting the Props—Discuss how to use the props in Doing the Book.
- Picture Walk—Confirm the actions and their sequence for Doing the Book.

**During:**
- Doing the Book—Pass out the props. The class choral reads the text while the characters pantomime the actions. Repeat allowing every child an opportunity to hold one of the props and participate in the pantomime.

**After:**
- Retelling—Select several children to tell about their "characters" and what happened to them in the story.

# Two-Day Format:

**Before:**
- Cover Talk and Picture Walk (See Day 1, page 11.)

**During:**
- Read Aloud (See Day 1, page 11.)
- Shared Reading (See Day 1, page 11.)

**After:**
- Discussion and Writing (See Day 2, page 11.)

**Before:**
- Picture Walk (See Day 1, page 11.)
- Finding and Writing (See Day 4, page 12.)

**During:**
- Choral Reading (See Day 4, page 12.)
- Finding and Writing (See Day 4, page 12.)

**After:**
- Completing the Cloze (See Day 4, page 12.)

# EXTENSIONS

**Predictable Chart Ideas:**

I found my lost sock _____.
I found my lost sock under my bed. (Mrs. Kim)
I found my lost sock in the closet. (Taylor)
I found my lost sock behind the TV. (Wesley)

My sock has _____.
My sock has polka dots. (Ms. Barfina)
My sock has lots of stripes. (Michael)
My sock has a bunny rabbit. (Vania)

**Read-Aloud Books:**
- *Dots, Spots, Speckles, and Stripes* by Tana Hoban (Greenwillow Books, 1987)
- *Caps For Sale* by Eshpyr Slobodkina (HarperTrophy, 1987)
- *Beep-Beep, Vroom, Vroom!* by Stuart J. Murphy (HarperTrophy, 2000)

# Across the Stream

## by Mirra Ginsburg
### (Scholastic Big Books, 1982)

A mother hen and her chicks have a dream that soon turns into a small nightmare. A hungry fox is following them. The dream does have a happy ending, thanks to a mother duck and her ducklings.

**Purpose:**
Build background knowledge and read for enjoyment.

**Before:**
- Building Background Knowledge and Making Connections—Ask, "Have you ever had a dream? What was the dream about? How did the dream end?" Announce that today's story is also about dreams.

**During:**
- Read Aloud—Read the book aloud to the students with full expression.
- Shared Reading—Invite students to join in and share the reading of the story.

**After:**
- Discussion—Have students summarize the hen's dream.

---

**Purpose:**
Use context, picture clues, and memory to Guess the Covered Word.

**Preparation/Materials Needed:**
- Place self-stick notes on the following words in the big book: **deep, three, kind, luck, dream, stream**.

**Before:**
- Retelling—Allow children to retell the story during a picture walk.

**During:**
- Reading to Guess the Covered Word—Choral read each page. In choral reading, the whole class reads the text with you or you can assign groups or parts to be read by different children. Take suggestions for the covered word, then uncover the beginning sound. Take additional suggestions if needed. Reveal the covered word, then reread the page.

**After:**
- Discussion—Talk about what happened in the story and how the students figured out the covered words.

© Carson-Dellosa CD-2422

## Purpose:
Identify the beginning, middle, and end of the story.
## Preparation/Materials Needed:
- Beach Ball with questions
- Three sentence strips
- Pocket chart with cards labeled: **Beginning, Middle, End**

**Before:**
- Retelling—Allow children to retell the story during a picture walk.

**During:**
- Echo Reading—Read a line and let the children be your echo, repeating the line after you. Have the children listen to see what happens in the story (beginning, middle, end).

**After:**
- Discussion and Writing—Ask, "What happened at the beginning? In the middle? At the end?" Write the responses on sentence strips and post them in the pocket chart.
- Beach Ball Questions—Toss the beach ball. Assist the student who catches the ball in reading one of the questions. Allow students to answer the question. Encourage students to refer to the pocket chart or book cover when giving their answers.

### EXAMPLE

**Beginning**
A fox is following the hen and her chicks.

**Middle**
Then, the hen and chicks run. They are trapped by a stream.

**End**
A duck and her ducklings help the hen and her chicks cross the stream.

---

## Purpose:
Read the story, find the rhyming words, and choose a spelling pattern to Make Words.
## Preparation/Materials Needed:
- Highlighting tape
- Highlight the following words: **luck, cluck** (page 13); **duck** (page 15); **kind, mind** (page 16); **quack, back** (page 17); **dream** (page 23); **stream** (page 24).
- Chart paper
- Letter vests or letters cards for the following rhyming pattern and beginning sounds: **-ack; t, r, p, b, l, c, s, n**

**Before:**
- Reviewing—Talk about rhyming words and any rhyming words the students heard in the story.
- Read Aloud—Have the children listen for rhyming words on pages 13, 15, 16, 17, 23, and 24.

**During:**
- Choral Reading—The whole class reads the text with you or you can assign groups or parts to be read by different children. Ask, "What did you notice today as we read the story? Which words rhymed?"

**After:**
- Finding and Writing—Find the rhyming words, then write them on the chart paper. If necessary, direct children to observe that there are pairs of words that rhyme using the same spelling pattern.
- Making Words the "Building-Blocks Way"—Pass out letter vests or cards for the spelling pattern **-ack, as in quack**. Have the three children with **a, c,** and **k** stand together at the front of the room as you blend the sounds. Then, pass out cards for **t, r, p, b, l, c, s,** and **n**. Guide the children with these cards to the front and have them stand with the **-ack** children to make new words using the spelling pattern and the other letter cards. Be sure that **c + r, t + r,** and **b + l** get together at the front, then blend their sounds together and make more words.

### EXAMPLE

| luck | kind | quack | stream |
| cluck | mind | back | dream |
| duck | | | |

**Purpose:**
   Participate in Doing the Book.
**Preparation/Materials Needed:**
   • The "Props"—cards with pictures or labels of the following: **hen**, **chick** (3); **duck**, **ducklings** (3); and **fox**

**Before:**
   • Presenting the Props—Show the props and discuss how to use them in Doing the Book.
   • Picture Walk—Take a picture walk through the book to confirm the actions and their sequence for Doing the Book.
**During:**
   • Doing the Book—Pass out the props. The class choral reads the text while the characters pantomime the actions.
   • Repeat, allowing every child an opportunity to participate in the pantomime.
**After:**
   • Writing and Drawing—Each student completes the following sentence: My favorite part of *Across the Stream* was _____. Then, have the students illustrate their sentences and share them with the class. The responses may be assembled into a class book as souvenirs (remembrances of the big book).

# Two-Day Format

**Before:**
   • Building Background Knowledge and Making Connections (See Day 1, page 14.)
**During:**
   • Read Aloud (See Day 1, page 14.)
   • Shared Reading (See Day 1, page 14.)
**After:**
   • Discussion and Writing (See Day 3, page 15.)
   • Beach Ball Questions (See Day 3, page 15.)

**Before:**
   • Picture Walk (See Day 1, page 14.)
**During:**
   • Choral Reading (See Day 4, page 15.)
**After:**
   • Finding and Writing (See Day 4, page 15.)
   • Making Words the "Building-Blocks Way" (See Day 4, page 15.)

**Read-Aloud Book:**
   • *Make Way for Ducklings* by Robert McCloskey (Viking Children's Books, 1976)

# Any Kind of Dog

## by Lynn Reiser
### (Harcourt School, 1992)

Richard wants a dog, any kind of dog. His mother, however, believes a dog would be too much trouble. She provides Richard with an assortment of other pets, but each one provides troubles of its own. Finally, Richard gets a dog, and, of course, the dog is too much trouble.

**Purpose:**
Build background knowledge and read for enjoyment.

**Before:**
- Building Background Knowledge and Making Connections—Read the first two-page spread of the text and share a childhood desire to have a dog or other pet. Allow the students to share similar experiences.
- Predictions—Predict if Richard can have a dog or not.

**During:**
- Reading and Thinking Aloud—After each two-page spread, pause and think aloud, "I wonder what Richard's mother will do now?" Allow students to give suggestions before turning the page.
- Shared Reading—Invite the students to join in and share the reading of the story.

**After:**
- Discussion—Ask, "What kind of trouble could a dog make?"

---

**Purpose:**
Discuss what this book is all about—a boy who wants a dog.

**Preparation/Materials Needed:**
- Highlighting tape

**Before:**
- Retelling—Allow students to retell the story during a picture walk.
- Predictions—Predict how many times the word **dog** will appear in the text.

**During:**
- Choral Reading—The whole class reads the text with the teacher or the teacher can assign groups or parts to be read by different children. Stop after each two-page spread. Allow students to find, highlight, and tally the word **dog**.

**After:**
- Discussion—Talk about why the word **dog** is used so many times (it is a story about a dog!). Ask, "What kind of dog did Richard want? What kind of dog did Richard get?"

**Purpose:**
 Read to find out what animals names are in the story besides **dog**.
**Preparation/Materials Needed:**
  • Highlighting tape

**Before:**
  • Retelling—Use the cover as a catalyst for retelling the story.
**During:**
  • Echo Reading—Read a line and let the children be your echo, repeating the line after you.
  • Choral Reading and Highlighting—The whole class reads the text with the teacher or the teacher can assign groups or parts to be read by different children. Stop after each two-page spread. Allow students to find and highlight the **names of animals**. Make sure to discuss with the students how they located the words.
**After:**
  • Discussion—Talk about how many other animals are in the big book. Ask, "What were the other animals in the book."

---

**Purpose:**
 Create a chart of animals and their dog look-alikes.
**Preparation/Materials Needed:**
  • Chart with the headings: **Animal, Dog Look-Alike**
  • Pictures of animals and dogs presented in the text of the big book

**Before:**
  • Reviewing—Ask, "What animals did Richard's mother give him?" List student responses in the **Animal** column of the chart.
**During:**
  • Choral Reading—Assign groups and choral read in two parts, alternating the reading of pages.
**After:**
  • Finding and Writing—Find the name of each dog look-alike and write it on the chart.
  • Extending the Chart—Match the pictures of the animals with their names on the chart.

---

**Purpose:**
 Participate in Doing the Book (acting out the story).
**Preparation/Materials Needed:**
  • The "Props"—pictures of the following: **caterpillar, mouse, baby alligator, lamb, pony, lion, bear, dog**. On the back of each picture, write the first line of text given for each animal in the text (for example, on the back of the caterpillar picture write, "so she gave him a caterpillar.").
  • Chart and pictures from Day 4

**Before:**
  • Reviewing—Match the animal pictures with their names on the chart from Day 4 (above).
**During:**
  • Doing the Book—Pass out the props. The class choral-reads the text while the characters pantomime the actions. Repeat, allowing every child an opportunity to participate in the pantomime.
**After:**
  • Writing and Drawing—Each student completes the sentence, "If I had a dog I would _____." Then, have the students illustrate their responses and share them with the class. The responses may then be accumulated into a class book or sent home as souvenirs (remembrances of the big book).

---

# Two-Day Format:

**Before:**
- Building Background Knowledge and Making Connections (See Day 1, page 17.)

**During:**
- Reading and Thinking Aloud (See Day 1, page 17.)
- Shared Reading (See Day 1, page 17.)

**After:**
- Discussion (See Day 2, page 17.)

**Before:**
- Picture Walk (See Day 1, page 17.)

**During:**
- Choral Reading (See Day 4, page 18.)
- Creating a Chart (See Day 4, page 18.)

**After:**
- Extending the Chart (See Day 4, page 18.)
- Writing and Drawing (See Day 5, page 18.)

### Predictable Chart Idea:
I want a _____ dog.
I want a <u>slow dog</u>. (Mr. Duane)
I want a <u>spotted dog</u>. (Cece)
I want a <u>hunting dog</u>. (Jimmie Lee)

### Field Trip Idea:
Visit a local pet shop, humane society, or veterinarian.

### Read-Aloud Books:
- *Arf! Beg! Catch! Dogs from A to Z* by Henry Horenstein (Scholastic, Inc., 1999)
- *Why Do Dogs Bark?* by Joan Holub (Penguin Putnam Books for Young Readers, 2001)
- *Surprise Puppy* by Judith Walker-Hodge (DK Publishing, 1998)

# As the Crow Flies
# A First Book of Maps

## by Gail Hartman
### (Macmillan/McGraw-Hill, 1991)

Follow an eagle, a rabbit, a crow, a horse, and a seagull as each animal travels to its favorite place. And just in case you get lost, each animal has a simple map to share with you.

**Purpose:**
Build background knowledge and read for enjoyment.

**Before:**
- Building Background Knowledge and Making Connections—Share some aerial photos. Discuss the places, objects, and roads in the photo. Next, share some simple maps and show how to follow a road on the map. Link the map and photo to each other if possible.
- Picture Talk—Use the picture map on pages 30 to 31 of the big book as a catalyst for discussion.

**During:**
- Read Aloud—Read the big book aloud to the students with full expression.
- Shared Reading—Invite the students to join in and share the reading of the story.

**After:**
- Discussion—Ask, "What are some of the places the animals liked to visit?"

---

**Purpose:**
List and categorize the names of buildings in the story.

**Preparation/Materials Needed:**
- Highlighting tape
- Highlight the following words: **farmhouse, shed, factory, houses, hot dog stand, skyscrapers**.
- Pocket chart
- Index cards

**Before:**
- Retelling—Allow students to retell the story during a picture walk.

**During:**
- Echo Reading—Read a line and let the children be your echo, repeating the line after you.

**After:**
- Finding and Writing—Find the highlighted words and write them on index cards. Encourage students to share the strategies they used to decode the words.
- Categorizing—Ask, "What did you notice about the list of words?" If necessary, direct the children to observe that the words are all names of buildings. Add the title **Buildings** to the top of the list.

### Purpose:
Highlight and write the names of places.
### Preparation/Materials Needed:
- Pocket chart from Day 2 (see page 20)
- Highlighting tape
- Pictures of a **crow**, an **eagle**, a **rabbit**, a **horse**, a **seagull**

**Before:**
- Retelling—Use the cover as a catalyst for retelling the story.
- Setting a Purpose for Reading—Say, "Yesterday we found names of buildings in the text. Today we will search for names of other places." Create a new pocket-chart column with the title **Places**.

**During:**
- Choral Reading and Highlighting—The whole class reads the text with you or you can assign parts to be read by different children. Stop after each two-page spread. Ask, "Are there any places named on these pages?" Allow students to highlight the place names in the text. Write these words on index cards and place the cards in the pocket chart.

**After:**
- Extending the Chart—Remove the place names from the pocket chart. Place the pictures of the animals in the pocket chart. Pass out the place name cards and have the students place them next to the appropriate animals. Use the maps in the book to check the students' choices.

---

### Purpose:
Read the story and use context, picture clues, and memory to Guess the Covered Word.
### Preparation/Materials Needed:
- Place self-stick notes on the following words: **meadow**, **shed**, **garden**, **factory**, **streets**, **park**, **harbor**.

**Before:**
- Retelling—Use the cover as a catalyst for retelling the story.

**During:**
- Choral Reading to Guess the Covered Word—The whole class reads the text with you or you can assign parts to be read by different children. Stop after each page. Take suggestions for the covered word and read the sentence using each suggested word. Reveal the beginning letter or letters, then take suggestions and read the sentence using each suggested word. Finally, reveal the covered word and reread the page.

**After:**
- Discussion—Talk about what happened in the story. Have students name the places in the story. Ask, "Was our retelling correct? Did we forget anything?"

---

### Purpose:
Retell each animal's path using a map and/or list.
### Preparation/Materials Needed:
- Word and picture cards from Day 3 (above)
- Pocket chart

**Before:**
- Reviewing—Place the pictures of the animals in the pocket chart. Pass out the place name cards. Have students put the place names next to the appropriate animals. Tell the students, "Let's read the story again to see if we are right."

---

**During:**
- Choral Reading—The whole class reads the text with the teacher or the teacher can assign groups or parts to be read by different children. Stop at the end of each animal's journey.

**After:**
- Sequencing—Close the book and have the students correctly sequence the journey taken by each animal. Use the map on pages 30-31 of the big book or the pocket chart from Day 2 (page 20) to check the sequence.

# Two-Day Format:

**Before:**
- Building Background Knowledge and Making Connections (See Day 1, page 20.)

**During:**
- Read Aloud (See Day 1, page 20.)
- Shared Reading (See Day 1, page 20.)

**After:**
- Finding and Writing (See Day 2, page 20.)

**Before:**
- Picture Walk (See Day 1, page 20.)

**During:**
- Guess the Covered Word (See Day 4, page 21.)
- Choral Reading (See Day 4, page 21.)

**After:**
- Sequencing (See Day 5, above.)

### Social Studies Connection:
This book provides an excellent opportunity to initiate a unit on maps.

### Read-Aloud Books:
- *Where Do I Live?* by Neil Chesanow (Barrons Educational Series, Inc., 1995)
- *Me on the Map* by Joan Sweeney (Crown Publishing Group, 1998)
- *Mapping Penny's World* by Loreen Leedy (Henry Holt Books for Young Readers, 2000)
- *Taxi: A Book of City Words* by Betsy and Giulio Maestro (Houghton Mifflin Co., 1989)

# Brown Bear, Brown Bear, What Do You See?

## by Bill Martin, Jr.
### (Harcourt Brace School, 1993)

This book's very predictable rhyme and simple, but delightful illustrations let children join the fun and, at the same time, become acquainted with some familiar animals and colors. All the children in the class will soon believe they are readers after just two or three readings of this classic book.

**Purpose:**
  Build background knowledge and read for enjoyment.

**Before:**
- Cover Talk—Ask, "What do you notice? What do you think this book is about? Why do you think the book is titled *Brown Bear, Brown Bear, What Do You See?*"

**During:**
- Read Aloud—Read the big book aloud to the students with full expression.
- Shared Reading—Invite the students to join in and share the reading of the story.

**After:**
- Discussion—Talk about the book. Ask, "What did you like about the book?"
- Dismissing by Task—Use the children's names in a similar rhyming pattern and let them tell what they see in the room, then dismiss them to their seats.

| | |
|---|---|
| Teacher: | Billy, Billy what do you see? |
| Billy: | I see a chalkboard. |
| Teacher: | Mary, Mary what do you see? |
| Mary: | I see my best friend. |

---

**Purpose:**
  Highlight the color words.
**Preparation/Materials Needed:**
- Highlighting tape

**Before:**
- Retelling—Let the students retell the story during a picture walk.

**During:**
- Choral Reading and Highlighting—The whole class reads the text with the teacher or the teacher can assign groups or parts to be read by different children. Stop after each page. Allow students to find and highlight the color words. Make sure to talk with the students about how they located the words.

**After:**
- Discussion—Talk about the highlighted words (color words) and why they are highlighted.

---

**Purpose:**
Use context, picture clues, and onset to Guess the Covered Word.

**Preparation/Materials Needed:**
- Place self-stick notes on the names of animals in the story
- Write the names of the animals on index cards. Place the index cards in the pocket chart.

**Before:**
- Retelling—Use the cover as a catalyst for retelling the story.

**During:**
- Choral Reading to Guess the Covered Word—The whole class reads the text with the teacher or the teacher can assign groups or parts to be read by different children. Stop after each page. Ask, "Who thinks they can find the covered word in the pocket chart?" Make sure to have the student explain the strategy used to determine his choice. Reveal the beginning letter or letters and discuss the student's choice. Then, uncover the word and reread the page.

**After:**
- Discussion—Talk about the questions on each page. Don't forget to talk about the students' answers, too.

---

**Purpose:**
Match the color words with the appropriate animal names.

**Preparation/Materials Needed:**
- Index cards of animal names from Day 3 (above)
- Index cards with the color words from the story
- Randomly place all of the index cards in a pocket chart.

**Before:**
- Match the Animals and Colors—Picture walk through the book, stopping at each two-page spread. Ask, "What animal is on this page?" Have a student locate the index card with the correct animal name on it. Ask, "What color is the animal on this page?" Have another student locate the index card with the color on it. Pair the animal name and color word together in the pocket chart.

**During:**
- Choral Reading—Assign groups and choral read in two parts. One group reads the question. The other group reads the response.

**After:**
- Matching the Animals and Colors—Mix up the index cards and have students match them. Use the book to check the pairings.

---

**Purpose:**
Participate in Doing the Book (acting out the story).

**Preparation/Materials Needed:**
- Index cards with the pictures of the animals featured in the big book
- On the back of the index cards, write the text describing what each animal sees. For example: brown bear/I see a red bird looking at me. red bird/I see a yellow duck looking at me.

**Before:**
- Discussion—Talk about how the "animals" will read their parts (written on the backs of the pictures). The other children will read the questions.

---

**During:**
- Doing the Book—Pass out the animal pictures. The students without the pictures will read the questions in the book. The students with the pictures will read the responses written on the backs of the pictures. Repeat allowing every child an opportunity to be an animal, use a picture, and participate in the pantomime.

**After:**
- Matching the Animals and Colors—Mix up the index cards and have students match them. Discuss whether each animal is really that color (for example, "Has anyone seen a purple cat?").

## Two-Day Format:

**Before:**
- Cover Talk (See Day 1, page 23.)

**During:**
- Read Aloud (See Day 1, page 23.)
- Shared Reading (See Day 1, page 23.)

**After:**
- Discussion (See Day 1, page 23.)

**Before:**
- Picture Walk (See Day 1, page 23.)

**During:**
- Doing the Book (See Day 5, above.)

**After:**
- Matching the Animals and Colors (See Day 5, above.)

### Predictable Chart Idea:

_____, _____what do you see? I see _____ looking at me.

Mr. Webman, Mr. Webman what do you see? I see Dottie looking at me.

Dottie, Dottie what do you see? I see Pat looking at me.

Pat, Pat what do you see? I see Joe looking at me.

### Read-Aloud Book:
- *Zoo-Looking* by Mem Fox (Mondo, 1996)

### Internet Sites:
**Lesson extensions:**

http://www.eric-carle.com/bb-bb.html

Reproducible mini-book with a similar format:

http://www.enchantedlearning.com/whatdoisay/

---

# Building a House

## by Byron Barton
### (Hampton Brown, 1992)

Building a house requires a lot of work and workers. This book's simple text and pictures present the many tools and jobs involved in building a house.

**Purpose:**
Build background knowledge and read for enjoyment.

**Before:**
- Cover Talk—Ask, "What do you notice? What is the man doing? Why do you think the story is titled *Building a House*? What could happen in this story?"
- Picture Walk—Start a discussion of each page with the question, "What do you notice?" Talk about the pictures and some important words.

**During:**
- Read Aloud—Read the big book aloud to the students with full expression.
- Shared Reading—Invite the students to join in and share the reading of the story.

**After:**
- Discussion—Ask, "What jobs have to be done to build a house?"

---

**Purpose:**
Use context, picture clues, and memory to Guess the Covered Word.

**Preparation/Materials Needed:**
- Place self-stick notes on the following words: **digs, hammer, roof, fireplace, pipes, lights, windows**.

**Before:**
- Retelling—Allow children to retell the story during a picture walk.

**During:**
- Reading to Guess the Covered Word—Choral read each page. Take students' suggestions for the covered word, then uncover the beginning letter or letters and see if any of the guesses begin with the correct letter and make sense. Let the students make more guesses, then reveal the covered word and reread the page.

**After:**
- Discussion—Talk about the story and the tools needed to build a house. Ask, "What parts does a house need?"

**Purpose:**
Highlight the names of workers.
**Preparation/Materials Needed:**
• Highlighting tape

**Before:**
• Retelling—Use the cover of the big book as a catalyst for retelling the story.
**During:**
• Echo Reading—Read a line and let the children be your echo, repeating the line after you.
• Choral Reading and Highlighting—The whole class reads the text with the teacher or the teacher can assign parts to be read by different children. Stop after each two-page spread. Allow students to find and highlight the names of workers. Make sure to talk with the students about how they located the word.
**After:**
• Discussion—Talk about the different workers in the book.

**Purpose:**
Write the names of workers and their jobs.
**Preparation/Materials Needed:**
• Chart paper

**Before:**
• Reviewing the Story—Find and list the names of workers you discussed on Day 3, in the order they appear in the story.
**During:**
• Choral Reading—The whole class reads the text with the teacher or the teacher can assign parts to be read by different children.
• Finding and Writing—Stop after each page with a highlighted word. Ask, "What job does this worker do?" Write the responses.
**After:**
• Discussion—Ask questions about the workers and their jobs. Have students locate the answers on the chart paper list. Ask, "Is our list complete?"

**EXAMPLE**

**builders**
hammer
saw

**cement mixer**
pours cement

**bricklayers**
lay large blocks
build the fireplace
build the chimney

**Purpose:**
Create a souvenir of the big book for each child to take home.
**Preparation/Materials Needed:**
• Graham crackers, canned frosting, and chocolate bars
• A small milk carton (rinsed) for each student
• Chart created on Day 4

**Before:**
• Discussion—Ask questions about workers and their jobs ("What do builders do? What do they need?").
**During:**
• Choral Reading—The whole class reads the text with the teacher or the teacher can assign parts to be read by different children.
**After:**
• Souvenirs—Make a house using the milk carton as a frame. Spread frosting on the milk carton and add graham crackers for the walls and roof. Use pieces of the chocolate bar for the door and windows. (Optional: Add gumdrops or other small candy pieces for decoration.) Send the souvenirs home and encourage the children to discuss the house and the story with their parents.

# Two-Day Format:

**Before:**
- Cover Talk and Picture Walk (See Day 1, page 26.)

**During:**
- Read Aloud (See Day 1, page 26.)
- Shared Reading (See Day 1, page 26.)

**After:**
- Finding and Writing (See Day 4, page 27.)

**Before:**
- Discussion (See Day 4, page 27.)

**During:**
- Choral Reading (See Day 4, page 27.)

**After:**
- Souvenirs (See Day 5, page 27.)

**Predictable Chart Idea:**
My house is _____.
My house is <u>made of brick</u>. (Mrs. Wood)
My house is <u>painted brown</u>. (Grace)
My house is <u>on Pine Street</u>. (Juan)

**Career Study:**
Study construction jobs.

**Field Trip:**
Visit a home construction site.

**Center:**
Allow children to build houses with building blocks.

**Read-Aloud Books:**
- *How a House Is Built* by Gail Gibbons (Holiday House, Inc., 1996)
- *Mike Mulligan and His Steam Shovel* by Virginia Burton (Houghton Mifflin Co., 1976)
- *Houses and Homes* by Ann Morris (William Morrow and Co., 1995)

(The following books are only available as part of a six-pack.)
- *Building a House* by Annette Smith, Jenny Giles, and Beverley Randell (Rigby, 2001)
- *Our New House* by Annette Smith, Jenny Giles, and Beverley Randell (Rigby, 2001)

# The Carrot Seed

## by Ruth Kraus
### (Scholastic Big Books, 1945)

A little boy plants a seed. Everyone tells him, "It won't come up." Despite the lack of encouragement, the boy continues to care for his seed. One day it finally comes up. It is a carrot, so big that it takes a wheelbarrow to get it home.

**Purpose:**
Build background knowledge and read for enjoyment.

**Before:**
- Cover Talk—Ask, "What do you notice? What is the boy doing? What will the boy need to do to grow the seed?"
- Picture Walk—Start a discussion of each page with the question, "What do you notice?" Talk about the pictures and new words (vocabulary) in the text.

**During:**
- Read Aloud—Read the big book aloud to the students with full expression.
- Shared Reading—Invite the students to join in and share the reading of the story.

**After:**
- Discussion—Ask, "What kind of seeds could you plant in a garden?" Responses can be placed on a web with the heading **Seeds**.

---

**Purpose:**
Identify the beginning, middle, and end of the story.

**Preparation/Materials Needed:**
- Beach Ball with questions
- Three sentence strips
- Pocket chart with header cards labeled: **Beginning**, **Middle**, **End**.

**Before:**
- Retelling—Allow children to retell the story during a picture walk.

**During:**
- Echo Reading—Read a line and let the children be your echo, repeating the line after you.

**After:**
- Discussion and Writing—Ask, "What happened at the beginning? In the middle? At the end?" Write students' responses on sentence strips and post them in the pocket chart.
- Beach Ball Questions—Toss the beach ball. Assist the student who catches the ball in reading one of the questions. Allow students to answer the question. Encourage them to refer to the pocket chart or book cover when giving their answers.

---

**EXAMPLE**

**Beginning**
The boy planted a seed.

**Middle**
The boy watered and cared for the seed.

**End**
The seed grew into a very big carrot.

---

© Carson-Dellosa CD-2422
*Shared Reading with Big Books*

**Purpose:**
Read the big book again and write a summary of the story.
**Preparation/Materials Needed:**
- Chart paper

**Before:**
- Retelling—Use the cover as a catalyst for retelling the story.

**During:**
- Choral Reading—The whole class reads the text with the teacher or the teacher can assign groups or parts to be read by different children.

**After:**
- Discussion—Talk about what happened at the beginning, in the middle, and at the end of the story.
- Summarizing—Write a summary of the big book with the class. Tell about the characters, setting, and what happened at the beginning, in the middle, and at end of the story.

**Purpose:**
Draw and write in response to reading.
**Preparation/Materials Needed:**
- Drawing paper and crayons

**Before:**
- Reviewing—Ask, "What happened to the seed in the story?" Have students tell how a seed grows. Then, read the story again to see if they are correct.

**During:**
- Choral Reading—Assign groups and choral read in two parts. One group only reads the words, "It won't come up." The other group reads the remaining text. Choral read again, but have the groups switch parts this time.

**After:**
- Discussion—Ask, "How would you grow a carrot seed?"
- Drawing and Writing—Each student draws a picture of a person planting a carrot seed and writes a sentence telling what is happening in the picture. Share the completed pieces with the class, then put them together to make a class book.

**Purpose:**
Participate in Doing the Book, eat a snack, and take home a souvenir.
**Preparation/Materials Needed:**
- The "Props"—labeled picture cards of **mom**, **dad**, **brother**, **little boy**
- Baby carrots
- Carrot seeds

**Before:**
- Presenting the Props—Talk about how to use them in Doing the Book.
- Picture Walk—Confirm the actions and their sequence for Doing the Book.

**During:**
- Doing the Book—Pass out the props. The class choral reads the text while the characters pantomime the actions. Repeat allowing every child to use the props and participate in the pantomime.

**After:**
- Souvenirs—Have a snack of baby carrots. Provide children with carrot seeds (place in snack-size resealable bags) to take home, along with instructions for growing the seeds.

# Two-Day Format:

**Before:**
- Cover Talk and Picture Walk (See Day 1, page 29.)

**During:**
- Read Aloud (See Day 1, page 29.)
- Shared Reading (See Day 1, page 29.)

**After:**
- Discussion and Writing (See Day 2, page 29.)

**Before:**
- Picture Walk (See Day 1, page 29.)

**During:**
- Choral Reading (See Day 3, page 30.)

**After:**
- Discussion (See Day 4, page 30.)
- Doing the Book (See Day 5, page 30.)

### Science:

Bring a whole carrot to class, leaves and all. They can be purchased year-round in small bunches at most grocery stores. Discuss the parts. Draw the carrot and label its parts.

Cut one inch off the top of the carrot. Remove the leaves and stand the top in a shallow container of water, so the water comes halfway up the carrot. Keep the carrot in the sun and top the water off daily. Make daily observations for two to three weeks.

### Read-Aloud Books:
- *Tops and Bottoms* by Janet Stevens (Harcourt Brace, 1995)
- *Vegetable Garden* by Douglas Florian (Voyager Books, 1996)

# Carry-Out Food

## by Andrea Butler
### (Rigby, 1987)

Have you ever been hungry, but did not want to prepare dinner? The solution is easy . . . carry-out food. That's what the family in this simple book is prepared to do. But what should they get to eat?

**Purpose:**
Build background knowledge and read for enjoyment.

**Before:**
- Cover Talk—Ask, "What do you notice? What is everybody pointing at? What are they talking about? What is carry-out food? What are some examples of carry-out food?"

**During:**
- Read Aloud—Read the book aloud to the students with full expression.
- Shared Reading—Invite the students to join in and share the reading of the story.

**After:**
- Discussion—Talk about the story, making sure to talk about the refrain. Send students back to their seats with this activity:

| | |
|---|---|
| Teacher: | Hey, red group, carry-out tonight. Do you want chicken? |
| Red Group: | No, not chicken! (And the red group goes back to their seats). |
| Teacher: | Hey, green group, carry-out tonight. Do you want tacos? |
| Green Group: | No, not tacos! (And the green group goes back to their seats). |

When all the groups have returned to their seats:

| | |
|---|---|
| Teacher: | What do you want to eat? |
| Students: | Everything! |

**Purpose:**
Highlight the names of food.
**Preparation/Materials Needed:**
- Highlighting tape

**Before:**
- Retelling—Allow students to retell the story during a picture walk.

**During:**
- Echo Reading—Read a line and let the children be your echo, repeating the line after you.
- Choral Reading and Highlighting—The whole class reads the text with you or you can assign parts to be read by different children. Stop after each page. Allow students to find and highlight the names of food. Make sure to talk with students about how they located the word.

**After:**
- Discussion—Talk about the foods the students highlighted in the story. Read the text again. The students will read the highlighted words (foods).
- Dismissal—Send the children back to their seats using the refrain from the After activity on Day 1.

**Purpose:**
Use context, picture clues, and onset to Guess the Covered Word.
**Preparation/Materials Needed:**
- Self-stick notes
- Place self-stick notes on the **names of food** the first time they appear in the story.

**Before:**
- Retelling—Use the cover as a catalyst for retelling the story.

**During:**
- Choral Reading to Guess the Covered Word—The whole class reads the text with you. Stop after each page. Take suggestions for the covered word, then uncover the beginning sound. Take additional suggestions if needed. Reveal the covered word, then reread the page.
- Choral Reading—Choral read in two parts. You read the mother's part. The students read the children's part.

**After:**
- Discussion—Talk about the food in the story. Ask, "Which of these foods do you eat? Which of these foods do you like? Which of these foods do you get to carry out?"

**Purpose:**
Correctly sequence events and write a summary of the story.
**Preparation/Materials Needed:**
- Chart paper labeled: **Beginning, Middle, End**
- Chart paper for summary

**Before:**
- Discussion and Writing—Ask, "What happened at the beginning? In the middle? At the end?" Write students' responses on the chart.

**During:**
- Choral Reading—Assign groups and choral read in two parts. You read the mother's part. The students read the children's part. Choral read again, but switch parts this time.

**After:**
- Summarizing—Write a summary of the big book with the class. Tell about the characters, setting, and what happened at the beginning, in the middle, and at end of the story.

**Purpose:**
Visit a fast-food restaurant or the school kitchen.
**Preparation/Materials Needed:**
- Chart paper

**Before:**
- Building Background Knowledge—Generate questions to ask at the restaurant or kitchen. Write them on the chart paper. Assign questions to various groups.

**During:**
- Field Trip—Go on the field trip, asking the chart-paper questions at the end of the trip.

**After:**
- Journal—Draw and write responses to the question, "What was the most interesting thing on our field trip?" Allow students to share their responses. Make a class book or bulletin board display with the responses.

## Two-Day Format:

**Before:**
- Cover Talk (See Day 1, page 32.)

**During:**
- Read Aloud (See Day 1, page 32.)
- Shared Reading (See Day 1, page 32.)

**After:**
- Discussion (See Day 1, page 32.)

**Before:**
- Picture Walk (See Day 1, page 32.)

**During:**
- Choral Reading to Guess the Covered Word (See Day 3, page 33.)

**After:**
- Summarizing (See Day 4, page 33.)

### Predictable Chart Idea:

I want to eat _____.
I want to eat <u>tacos</u>. (Mrs. Clock)
I want to eat <u>at Hamburger Hut</u>. (Nina)
I want to eat <u>pizza</u>. (Keith)

### Important Words:

Have students bring in bags from their favorite fast-food restaurants. Link this story to environmental print activities based on restaurants.

### Interactive Chart:

Rewrite the story, replacing the food words, and then illustrate the story. For example:

It's snack time. What do you want to eat?
A candy bar ?
No, not a candy bar .
Chocolate milk ?
No, not chocolate milk .
You don't want a candy bar .
You don't want chocolate milk .
What do you want?
EVERYTHING!

### Read-Aloud Book:

- *What Would You Like?* by Joy Cowley (Wright Group, 1989)
  Available only as a big book or in a six-pack.

# Chickens

## by Diane Snowball
### (Mondo, 1995)

The life cycle of the chicken, from egg to hen or rooster, is introduced. The simple text and illustrations provide an excellent foundation for the study of egg-laying animals.

**Purpose:**
Build background knowledge and read for enjoyment.

**Preparation/Materials Needed:**
- Chart paper labeled as KWL chart

| EXAMPLE | | |
|---|---|---|
| K | W | L |
| | | |

**Before:**
- Cover Talk—Ask, "What do you notice?"
- Start KWL—Ask, "What do you know about chickens?" Write students' responses in the **Know** (K) column of the KWL chart. When students cannot come to an agreement about a statement, create a question to place in the **Want to Learn** or **Wonder** (W) column.

**During:**
- Read Aloud—Read the big book aloud to the students with full expression.
- Shared Reading—Invite the students to join in and share the reading of the story.

**After:**
- Listing—List the things the children learned under the **Learned** (L) column of the KWL chart.

---

**Purpose:**
Use context, picture clues, and memory to Guess the Covered Word.

**Preparation/Materials Needed:**
- Place self-stick notes on the following words the first time they appear in the text: **rooster**, **hen**, **chickens**, **eggs**, **shells**.

**Before:**
- Retelling—Allow students to retell the story during a picture walk.

**During:**
- Choral Reading to Guess the Covered Word—The whole class reads the text with you or you can assign parts to be read by different children. Stop after each page. Take suggestions for the covered word, then uncover the beginning sound. Take additional suggestions if needed. Reveal the covered word, then reread the page.

**After:**
- Discussion—Talk with the children about the story and the important words.

## Purpose:

Create categories for the highlighted words.

## Preparation/Materials Needed:

- Highlighting tape
- Highlight the following words: **rooster, hen, chickens, eggs, four, fourteen, twenty-one, beaks, hatch.**
- Pocket chart
- Index cards

### Before:

- Retelling—Use the cover as a catalyst for retelling the story.

### During:

- Choral Reading—Assign groups and choral read in two parts. One group reads only the highlighted text. The other group reads the remaining text. Choral read again, but have the groups switch parts this time.

### After:

- Finding and Writing—Find the highlighted words, then write them on index cards. Encourage students to share the strategies they used to decode the words.
- Categorizing—Ask, "What do you notice about the list of words?" Encourage students to place words into categories. (For example: A hen is a female chicken and a rooster is a male chicken. Hatch and hen begin with **h**.)

---

## Purpose:

List the steps of hatching a chick.

## Preparation/Materials Needed:

- Sentence strips
- Pocket chart

| How to Hatch a Chick |
| :--- |
| 1. A hen and rooster mate. |
| 2. The hen lays an egg. |
| 3. The hen keeps the egg warm. |
| 4. The egg hatches in 21 days. |
| 5. The chick grows to be a hen or a rooster. |

### Before:

- Discussion and Writing—Ask, "How does a chick hatch from an egg?" Write the suggestions on sentence strips. Discuss each sentence strip and whether it should be placed at the beginning, in the middle, or at the end of the pocket chart. Finally, place the sentence strip in the pocket chart.

### During:

- Choral Reading—The whole class reads the text with you or you can assign groups or parts to be read by different children. Stop at the end of each two-page spread. Ask, "What happened on the page? Is this something we should add to our chart?" Write any new steps on sentence strips and add them to the pocket chart.

### After:

- Extending the Chart —Number the list and discuss the sequence of events.

---

## Purpose:

Reread the book and review the KWL chart created on Day 1.

## Preparation/Materials Needed:

- KWL chart from Day 1 (page 35) and the pocket chart from Day 4 (above)
- Any read-aloud books used to support the study of the life cycle of chickens.

**Before:**
- Reviewing—Choral read the pocket chart created on Day 4 (page 36). The whole class reads the pocket chart with you or you can assign parts to be read by different children.

**During:**
- Choral Reading—The whole class reads the big book with you or you can assign parts to be read by different children.

**After:**
- Completing the KWL—Ask, "What new things did you learn about chickens and chicks? Did we miss any?" Write any additional responses in the **Learn** (L) column and encourage students to discuss where they obtained the new information.

---

# Two-Day Format:

**Before:**
- Cover Talk (See Day 1, page 35.)
- Start KWL (See Day 1, page 35.)

**During:**
- Read Aloud (See Day 1, page 35.)

**After:**
- Listing (See Day 1, page 35.)

**Before:**
- Picture Walk (See Day 1, page 35.)

**During:**
- Choral Reading (See Day 5, above.)

**After:**
- Discussion and Writing (See Day 4, page 36.)

# EXTENSIONS

**Predictable Chart Idea:**

My egg will hatch and be a(n) _____.
My egg will hatch and be an <u>alligator</u>. (Mrs. Reid)
My egg will hatch and be a <u>frog</u>. (Alexandria)
My egg will hatch and be a <u>bird</u>. (Virginia)

**Read-Aloud Books:**
- *Horton Hatches an Egg* by Dr. Seuss (Random House, 1976)
- *Peeping Beauty* by Mary Jane Auch (Holiday House, Inc., 1993)
- *The Easter Egg Farm* by Mary Jane Auch (Holiday House, Inc., 1996)
- *Egg to Chick* by Millicent Ellis Selsom (HarperTrophy, 1987)
- *Chick: Watch Me Grow!* by Nancy Sheehan (Penguin, 2000)
- *The Chicken or the Egg* by Allan Fowler (Children's Press, 1993)

# Cookie's Week

## by Cindy Ward
### (Scholastic Big Books, 1988)

Each day of the week, Cookie, a lovable cat, finds a new place and a new way to get into trouble.

**Purpose:**
Build background knowledge and read for enjoyment.

**Before:**
- Building Background Knowledge and Making Connections—Ask, "Do any of you have pets? Do they ever get in trouble? What kind of trouble does your pet get into?"
- Cover Talk—Ask, "What do you notice? What is the cat's name? What do you think will happen in the story?"
- Picture Walk—Start a discussion of each page with the question, "What do you notice?" Talk with the children about important words.

**During:**
- Read Aloud—Read the big book aloud to the students with full expression.
- Shared Reading—Invite the students to join in and share the reading of the story.

**After:**
- Discussion—Talk about the days of the week and what happens to Cookie. Conclude with a song or rhyme about the days of the week.

---

**Purpose:**
Discuss and list the highlighted days of the week.

**Preparation/Materials Needed:**
- Highlighting tape
- Highlight the days of the week in the big book.
- Pocket chart and index cards
- Days of the week chart or poster

**Before:**
- Retelling—Allow students to retell the story during a picture walk.

**During:**
- Echo Reading—Read a line and let the children be your echo, repeating the line after you.

**After:**
- Finding and Writing—Find the highlighted words, then write them on index cards. Encourage the students to share the strategies they used to decode the words. Place the cards in the pocket chart.
- Sequencing Game—Mix up the index cards. Pass them out to seven students. Allow the students to arrange themselves in the correct order. Use a rhyme or poster to help if needed. Repeat the game until all students have had a chance to play.

**Purpose:**
Find and write the places Cookie was found.

**Preparation/Materials Needed:**
- Chart paper with three columns labeled: **Day of the Week, Where's Cookie?, What Happened?**
- Highlighting tape

**Before:**
- Retelling—Use the cover as a catalyst for retelling the story.
- Listing—Write the days of the week on the chart. Tell the students, "Let's read to find out where Cookie was on these days."

**During:**
- Choral Reading and Highlighting—The whole class reads the text with you or you can assign parts to be read by different children. Stop on any page with a day of the week in the text. Ask, "Where's Cookie?" Have a student use a pointer to locate the day in the text and write the answer on the chart.

**After:**
- Extending the Chart—Discuss the story and model how to retell the story using the chart. Allow some students to retell the story. It is helpful to use a pointer during the retelling.

---

**Purpose:**
Find and write what happened each day of the week.

**Preparation/Materials Needed:**
- Highlighting tape
- Three-column chart from Day 3

**Before:**
- Retelling—Retell the story using the chart from Day 3 (above).

**During:**
- Choral Reading and Highlighting—The whole class reads the text with you or you can assign parts to be read by different children. Stop on any page with a day of the week in the text. Ask, "What happened?"

**After:**
- Completing the Chart—Discuss the story. Ask, "What happened each day?" Have a student use a pointer to locate what happened in the text and write it on the chart. When the chart is complete, model how to retell the story using the chart. Allow some students to retell the story. It may be helpful to use a pointer during the retelling.

| EXAMPLE | | |
|---|---|---|
| Day of the Week | Where's Cookie? | What happened? |
| Monday | toilet | water everywhere |
| Tuesday | windowsill | dirt everywhere |
| Wednesday | trash | garbage everywhere |
| Thursday | drawer | pans everywhere |
| Friday | closet | clothes everywhere |
| Saturday | curtains | Cookie everywhere |
| Sunday | ? | rest...maybe? |

---

**Purpose:**
Participate in Doing the Book and predict a possible ending.

**Preparation/Materials Needed:**
- The "Props"—Cut up the words and phrases from the chart created on Days 3 and 4 (above).

---

**39**

*Shared Reading with Big Books*

**Before:**
- Predictions—Predict what Cookie will do on Sunday. The students write their predictions on paper.
- Presenting the Props—Discuss how to use them in Doing the Book. Students with the corresponding answers will stand up while their day of the week is read.
- Picture Walk—Confirm the actions and their sequence for Doing the Book.

**During:**
- Doing the Book—Pass out the props. The class choral reads the text while the characters pantomime the actions. Repeat until every child has a chance to participate in the pantomime.

**After:**
- Sharing—Allow students to tell the sequence of events. Ask, "What was your favorite day? What was your favorite place?" Be sure to let several students share.

# Two-Day Format:

**Before:**
- Cover Talk and Picture Walk (See Day 1, page 38.)

**During:**
- Read Aloud (See Day 1, page 38.)
- Shared Reading (See Day 1, page 38.)

**After:**
- Finding and Writing (See Day 2, page 38.)

**Before:**
- Picture Walk (See Day 1, page 38.)

**During:**
- Echo Reading (See Day 2, page 38.)

**After:**
- Finding and Writing/Listing (See Day 2, page 38 and Day 3, page 39.)

**Read-Aloud Books:**
- *All through the Week with Cat and Dog* by Rozanne L. Williams (Creative Teaching Press, Inc., 1995)
- *Today Is Monday* by Eric Carle (Philomel, 1993)

# Dinosaurs, Dinosaurs

## by Byron Barton
### (HarperCollins, 1989)

The prehistoric beasts with the long names are introduced to children through simple text and bold illustrations. The text explores the traits and characteristics of a wide variety of dinosaurs. This book is an excellent anchor for a class study of dinosaurs.

**Purpose:**
Build background knowledge and read for enjoyment.

| EXAMPLE | | |
|---|---|---|
| K | W | L |
| | | |

**Preparation/Materials Needed:**
- Chart paper and headings for a KWL chart

**Before:**
- Cover Talk—Ask, "What do you notice?"
- Starting KWL Chart—Ask, "What do you know about dinosaurs?" Write student responses in the **Know** (K) column of the KWL chart. When the students cannot come to an agreement about a statement, create a question to be placed in the **Want to Learn** or **Wonder** (W) column.

**During:**
- Read Aloud—Read the big book aloud to the students with full expression.
- Shared Reading—Invite the students to join in and share the reading of the story.

**After:**
- Completing KWL Chart—Ask, "What new things did you learn about dinosaurs?" Write the responses in the **Learned** (L) column and encourage students to discuss where they obtained the new information. Make sure to update the KWL after every activity that supports the dinosaur study.

---

**Purpose:**
To find out what this big book is all about (dinosaurs) by highlighting the word **dinosaur** and reading to find out what dinosaurs did.

**Preparation/Materials Needed:**
- Highlighting tape

**Before:**
- Retelling—Allow students to retell the story during a picture walk.
- Predictions—Predict how many times the word **dinosaur** will appear in the text.

**During:**
- Choral Reading and Highlighting—The whole class reads the text with you or you can assign parts to be read by different children. Stop after each two-page spread. Allow students to find, highlight, and tally the word **dinosaur**.

**After:**
- Discussion—Talk about the story and how many times the word dinosaur appeared in the text and why. Ask, "What did you learn about dinosaurs?"

**Purpose:**

Use context, picture clues and memory to Guess the Covered Word and find the words used to describe dinosaurs in the book.

**Preparation/Materials Needed:**

- Place self-stick notes on the following words: **horns**, **spikes**, **clubs**, **teeth**, **necks**
- KWL chart from Day 1

**Before:**

- Reviewing—Reflect back to the KWL chart started on Day 1 (page 41).

**During:**

- Reading to Guess the Covered Word—Choral read each page. The whole class reads the text with you or you can assign parts to be read by different children. Take suggestions for the covered word, then uncover the beginning sound. Take additional suggestions if needed. Reveal the covered word, then reread the page.

**After:**

- Discussion—Talk about the words that were used to describe dinosaur body parts in this book: **horns**, **spikes**, **clubs**, **teeth**, **neck**, etc.

---

**Purpose:**

Match pictures of dinosaurs to the correct descriptions.

**Preparation/Materials Needed:**

- Pictures of the following dinosaurs: **triceratops**, **kentrosaurus**, **ankylosaurus**, **stegosaurus**, **pachycephalosaurus**, **tyrannosaurus rex**
- Post the pictures on a bulletin board.
- Sentence strips
- KWL chart from Day 1

**Before:**

- Reviewing—Review information added to the KWL chart (page 41) and the pictures of the dinosaurs on the bulletin board (page 41).

**During:**

- Choral Reading—The whole class reads the text with you or you can assign parts to be read by different children.
- Matching—Read descriptions of dinosaurs from the big book text. Have students locate the pictures of the correct dinosaurs on the bulletin board.

**After:**

- Summarizing—Together with the children, write a brief description of each picture on a sentence strip (for example: This is a stegosaurus. The stegosaurus has spikes.).

---

**Purpose:**

Create a souvenir for this book and participate in Doing the Book.

**Preparation/Materials Needed:**

- White bulletin board paper
- Transparencies of the simple dinosaur drawings (See preparation for Day 4 drawings above.)
- Use overhead transparencies to create large (9" x 12" or 18" x 24") outlines of dinosaurs. Cut out the outlines. Each child will need two of the same dinosaur. If this task is too overwhelming, create one large dinosaur (18" x 24") for the class souvenir and smaller ones (9" x 12") for each child in the class.
- Tempera paints

---

**Before:**

- Modeling—Create a souvenir of a stuffed dinosaur. Model for the class how to make the souvenir by stapling together three sides of the dinosaur. Stuff crumpled or shredded paper inside. Staple together the remaining side. Paint the dinosaur with tempera paint. (You can create simple dinosaur silhouettes, if desired.)

**During:**

- Doing the Book—The class choral reads the text. Each student stands up with his stuffed dinosaur (or silhouette) when it is described in the text.

**After:**

- Souvenirs—Students create their own dinosaurs by following your model and step-by-step directions.

## Two-Day Format:

**Before:**

- Starting KWL Chart (See Day 1, page 41.)

**During:**

- Read Aloud (See Day 1, page 41.)
- Shared Reading (See Day 1, page 41.)

**After:**

- Completing KWL Chart (See Day 1, page 41.)

**Before:**

- Reviewing (See Day 3, page 42.)

**During:**

- Choral Reading (See Day 4, page 42.)

**After:**

- Matching (See Day 4, page 42.)
- Souvenirs (See Day 5, above.)

### Predictable Chart Idea:

Dinosaurs are _____.
Dinosaurs are <u>interesting</u>. (Ms. Door)
Dinosaurs are <u>dead</u>. (Shaquille)
Dinosaurs are <u>big</u>. (Kendra)

### Read-Aloud Books:

- *How Big Were the Dinosaurs?* by Bernard Most (Voyager Books, 1995)
- *Bones, Bones, Dinosaur Bones* by Byron Barton (Ty Crowell Co., 1990)
- *Digging Up Dinosaurs* by Aliki (HarperTrophy, 1988)
- *Dinosaur Time* by Peggy Parish (HarperCollins, 1974)

# The Doorbell Rang

## by Pat Hutchins
### (Scholastic Big Books, 1986)

A dozen cookies are enough for two, but the doorbell rings and then there are four. Again and again the doorbell rings and soon there are twelve. What will happen when the doorbell rings one more time?

**Purpose:**
Build background knowledge and read for enjoyment.

**Before:**
- Cover Talk—Ask, "What do you notice? What are the children doing? Why do you think the story is titled The Doorbell Rang? What could happen in this story?"
- Picture Walk—First page only—Ask, "What do you notice? What could happen in this story?"
- Build Background Knowledge and Make Connections—Create a web of different kinds of cookies (see example).

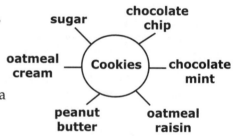

**During:**
- Read Aloud—Read the big book aloud to the students with full expression.
- Shared Reading —Invite the students to join in and share the reading of the story.

**After:**
- Writing and Drawing—The students should complete the following sentence and add an illustration: "I think my grandma would bring _____ cookies." Share the completed student responses.

---

**Purpose:**
Read the story again and talk about some of the important vocabulary words: **grandma**, **cookies**, **doorbell**.

**Preparation/Materials Needed:**
- Highlighting tape (If possible, use three different colors.)

**Before:**
- Retelling—Use the cover as a catalyst for retelling the story.

**During:**
- Echo Reading—Read a line and let the children be your echo, repeating the line after you.
- Choral Reading and Highlighting—The whole class reads the text with you or you can assign parts to be read by different children. Stop after each two-page spread. Allow students to find, highlight, and tally the vocabulary words.

**After:**
- Discussion—Talk about the story and what happened each time the doorbell rang. Discuss the highlighted words.

**Purpose:**
Find and write the total number of people and how many cookies each person gets.

| EXAMPLE | | |
|---|---|---|
| Total Number of Cookies | Number of People | Each person gets . . . |
| twelve | | |
| twelve | | |
| twelve | | |
| twelve | | |

**Preparation/Materials Needed:**
- Chart paper with three columns labeled as in the example.

**Before:**
- Retelling—Use the cover as a catalyst for retelling the story.
- New Idea—Introduce the concept of **dozen**. Write **twelve** in the total number of cookies column.

**During:**
- Choral Reading and Highlighting—The whole class reads the text with you or you can assign parts to be read by different children. Stop at appropriate times to gather information to complete the chart.

**After:**
- Extending the Chart—Create other hypothetical situations to add to the chart.

---

**Purpose:**
Create a script with your students for Doing the Book.
**Preparation/Materials Needed:**
- Chart paper

| EXAMPLE | |
|---|---|
| Ma: | "I've made some cookies for tea," |
| Narrator: | said Ma. |
| Victoria: | "Good!" |
| Sam: | "We're starving," |
| Narrator: | said Victoria and Sam. |
| Ma: | "Share them between yourselves. I made plenty," |
| Narrator: | said Ma. |

**Before:**
- Retelling—Allow students to retell the story.

**During:**
- Choral Reading—Assign groups and choral read in two parts. One group reads the dialogue. The other group reads the narration.

**After:**
- Writing a Script—Using the big book text, create a script with your students. Write the script on chart paper.

---

**Purpose:**
Participate in Doing the Book.
**Preparation/Materials Needed:**
- Cookies for the class
- Scripts from Day 4 (Make copies for the entire class.)

**Before:**
- Reviewing—Talk about the script and how you will use it in Doing the Book.

**During:**
- Doing the Book—Pass out the scripts and assign parts. The students who are not specific characters are narrators. Practice several times, adding actions and props.

**After:**
- Discussion—Talk about the sequence of events (who spoke first, next, etc.).

---

45

## Two-Day Format:

**Before:**
- Cover Talk and Picture Walk (See Day 1, page 44.)

**During:**
- Read Aloud (See Day 1, page 44.)
- Shared Reading (See Day 1, page 44.)

**After:**
- Discussion (See Day 2, page 44.)

**Before:**
- Picture Walk (See Day 1, page 44.)
- Writing a Script (See Day 4, page 45.)

**During:**
- Doing the Book (See Day 5, page 45.)

**After:**
- Discussion (See Day 5, page 45.)

# EXTENSIONS

**Present to an Audience:**
Invite another class to see the production. Serve cookies to everyone at the end of the show.

**Math:**
*The Doorbell Rang* provides an excellent opportunity to demonstrate the concept of division.

**Read-Aloud Books:**
- *Divide and Ride* by Stuart J. Murphy (Scott Foresman, 1997)
- *Spunky Monkeys on Parade* by Stuart J. Murphy (HarperTrophy, 1999)

# The Enormous Watermelon

## retold by Brenda Parkes and Judith Smith
### (Rigby, 1986)

A watermelon seed planted by Old Mother Hubbard grows and grows. It is so enormous that Mother Hubbard must enlist the help of some familiar characters, including Humpty Dumpty.

**Purpose:**
Build background knowledge and read for enjoyment.

**Preparation/Materials Needed:**
- Chart paper
- Write the nursery rhyme "Old Mother Hubbard" on chart paper.

**Before:**
- Building Background Knowledge and Making Connections—Talk with the class about eating watermelon. Allow students to share their own experiences.
- Cover Talk—Ask, "What do you notice? Who is that lady?"
- New Idea—Introduce the nursery rhyme "Old Mother Hubbard."
- Picture Walk—Start a discussion of each page with the questions, "What do you notice?" and "Who do you think the new character is on this page?" Talk about some important words and how pictures and sounds helped you figure them out.

**During:**
- Read Aloud—Read the big book aloud to the students with full expression.
- Shared Reading—Invite the students to join in and share the reading of the story.

**After:**
- Discussion—Talk about who Old Mother Hubbard is and what she does in the story. Then, choral read the nursery rhyme "Old Mother Hubbard."

---

**Purpose:**
Discuss the characters in this story and highlight each of the character names.

**Preparation/Materials Needed:**
- Highlighting tape
- Pocket chart
- Index cards

**Before:**
- Retelling—Allow students to retell the story during a picture walk.
- Reviewing—Ask, "Who was pulling the watermelon?" Write the students' responses on index cards and place the cards in the pocket chart.

**During:**
- Choral Reading and Highlighting—The whole class reads the text with you or you can assign parts to be read by different children. Stop after each two-page spread. Allow students to find and highlight any character names. Write and post any names that were not already in the pocket chart.

**After:**
- Discussion—Talk about the characters and what they do in the story.

---

## Purpose:
Identify the beginning, middle, and end of the story.

## Preparation/Materials Needed:
- Beach Ball with questions
- Three sentence strips
- Pocket chart with cards labeled: **Beginning, Middle, End**

**Before:**
- Retelling—Use the cover as a catalyst for retelling the story.

**During:**
- Echo Reading—Read a line and let the children be your echo, repeating the line after you.

**After:**
- Discussion and Writing—Ask, "What happened at the beginning? In the middle? At the end?" Write the students' responses on sentence strips and post them in the pocket chart.
- Beach Ball Questions—Toss the beach ball. Assist the student who catches the ball in reading one of the questions. Allow students to answer the question. Encourage them to refer to the pocket chart or book cover when giving their answers.

| EXAMPLE |
| --- |
| **Beginning**<br>Old Mother Hubbard grew an enormous watermelon.<br><br>**Middle**<br>Everyone helped to get the watermelon home.<br><br>**End**<br>They all ate pieces of watermelon. |

## Purpose:
Summarize and draw what happened in the book.

## Preparation/Materials Needed:
- Pocket chart from Day 3
- 9" x 12" drawing paper (or notebooks)

**Before:**
- Reviewing—Using the pocket chart created on Day 3 (above), talk about what happened in the story. Then, choral read the pocket chart. The whole class reads the chart with you or you can assign parts to be read by different children.

**During:**
- Choral Reading—The whole class reads the big book with you or you can assign parts to be read by different children.

**After:**
- Summarizing and Drawing—Have the children tell you in a sentence what happened to the watermelon seed. Then, let them draw a picture to illustrate the sentence.

## Purpose:
Participate in Doing the Book.

## Preparation/Materials Needed:
- The "Props"—illustrations of **Old Mother Hubbard, Little Miss Muffet, Jack and Jill,** and **Wee Willy Winky** (cards labeled Old Mother Hubbard, Little Miss Muffet, etc., will work.)
- A ball to use as a watermelon
- Fresh watermelon for students to eat

**Before:**
- Presenting the Props—Discuss how to use them in Doing the Book.
- Picture Walk—Confirm the actions and their sequence for Doing the Book.

**During:**
- Doing the Book—Pass out the props. The class choral reads the text while the characters pantomime the actions. Repeat allowing every child to participate in the pantomime.

**After:**
- Discussion—Talk about the story. Then, let everyone eat watermelon and save the seeds. Send the seeds home in a snack-size, resealable plastic bag along with instructions on how to grow a watermelon plant.

# Two-Day Format:

**Before:**
- Cover Talk and Picture Walk (See Day 1, page 47.)

**During:**
- Read Aloud (See Day 1, page 47.)
- Shared Reading (See Day 1, page 47.)

**After:**
- Discussion and Writing (See Day 3, page 48.)

**Before:**
- Retelling (See Day 3, page 48.)

**During:**
- Choral Reading (See Day 4, page 48.)

**After:**
- Retelling (See Day 2, page 47.)
- Discussion (See Day 5, above.)

### Predictable Chart Idea:
I want to grow a big _____ to eat.
I want to grow a big <u>tomato</u> to eat. (Mr. Zee)
I want to grow a big <u>carrot</u> to eat. (Tom)
I want to grow a big <u>apple</u> to eat. (Beth)

### Thematic Tie-Ins:
Use the story as part of a study of nursery rhymes or folk tales.

### Math:
Predicting how many seeds are in a watermelon; counting watermelon seeds; grouping (tens and ones)

### Internet Sites:
Coloring pictures, rebus rhymes, games and activities
    http://www.enchantedlearning.com/Rhymes.html

Nursery rhymes
    http://www-personal.umich.edu/~pfa/dreamhouse/nursery/rhymes/

# The Farm Concert

## by Joy Cowley
### (Wright Group, 1998)

A farm is filled with many wonderful sounds. Wonderful, if you don't mind a little noise. However, it's nighttime and the farmer would like to sleep. He demands quiet and the animals do their best to let the farmer sleep.

**Purpose:**
Build background knowledge and read for enjoyment.

**Preparation/Materials Needed:**
- Chart paper
- Draw a web on chart paper like the example

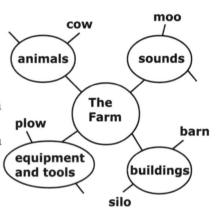

**Before:**
- Building Background Knowledge and Making Connections—Introduce the categories of the web and have the students suggest additions. Write the student responses in the appropriate places on the web (see example).
- Picture Walk—First half of the book only. Start a discussion of each page with the question, "What do you notice?"

**During:**
- Read Aloud—Read the big book aloud to the students with full expression.
- Shared Reading— Invite the students to join in and share the reading of the story.

**After:**
- Discussion—Talk about what happened in the story.

---

**Purpose:**
Identify the beginning, the middle, and the end of the story.

**Preparation/Materials Needed:**
- Beach Ball with questions
- Three sentence strips
- Pocket chart with cards labeled: **Beginning, Middle, End**

**Before:**
- Retelling—Allow children to retell the story during a picture walk.

**During:**
- Echo Reading—Read a line and let the children be your echo, repeating the line after you.

**After:**
- Discussion and Writing—Ask, "What happened at the beginning? In the middle? At the end?" Write the students' responses on sentence strips and place them in the pocket chart.
- Beach Ball Questions—Toss the beach ball. Assist the students in reading a question on the ball. Allow students to answer the question. Encourage them to refer to the pocket chart or book cover when giving their answers.

**Purpose:**
Use context, picture clues, and onset to Guess the Covered Word.
**Preparation/Materials Needed:**
* Self-stick notes
* Place self-stick notes on the **names of animals** in the story

**Before:**
* Retelling—Use the cover as a catalyst for retelling the story.

**During:**
* Choral Reading to Guess the Covered Word—The whole class reads the text with you. Stop after each page. Take suggestions for the covered word, then uncover the beginning sound. Take additional suggestions if needed. Reveal the covered word, then reread the page.

**After:**
* Discussion—Talk about the story and the uncovered words (animal names).

---

**Purpose:**
Match the animal names with the appropriate sounds.
**Preparation/Materials Needed:**
* Index cards with the headings **Animal** and **Sounds** and with the animal names and sounds (one animal or sound per card)
* Randomly place all the index cards in a pocket chart.

**Before:**
* Matching the Animals and Sounds—Picture walk through the book, stopping at each two-page spread. Ask, "What animal is on this page?" Have a student locate the index card with the animal's name on it. Ask, "What sound does the animal on this page make?" Have another student locate the index card with the animal's sound on it. Pair the animal name and sound in the pocket chart.

**During:**
* Choral Reading—Assign groups and choral read in two parts. One group reads the animal sounds. The other group reads the remaining text. Read to find out if the pairings were correct.

**After:**
* Extending the Chart—Mix up the index cards and have students match each animal name with its sound. Use the book to check the pairings, if necessary.

---

**Purpose:**
Participate in Doing the Book.
**Preparation/Materials Needed:**
* The "Props"— illustrations of a **farmer**, **cow**, **dog**, **duck**, **frog**, **pig**, **sheep**
* Animal crackers in small snack-size bags

**Before:**
* Presenting the Props—Discuss how to use the props in Doing the Book.

**During:**
* Doing the Book—Pass out the props. The class choral reads the text while the characters pantomime the actions and make the appropriate sounds. Repeat allowing every child to participate in the pantomime.

**After:**
* Discussion—Talk about the story, who spoke, and what happened, then pass out the bags of animal crackers for a snack, or as a take-home souvenir of the story.

# Two-Day Format:

**Before:**
- Web (See Day 1, page 50.)
- Picture Walk (See Day 1, page 50.)

**During:**
- Read Aloud (See Day 1, page 50.)
- Shared Reading (See Day 1, page 50.)

**After:**
- Discussion and Writing (See Day 2, page 50.)

**Before:**
- Matching the Animals and Sounds (See Day 4, page 51.)

**During:**
- Choral Reading to Guess the Covered Word (See Day 3, page 51.)

**After:**
- Doing the Book (See Day 5, page 51.)

### Predictable Chart Idea:

A _____ likes to _____.
A <u>cow </u>likes to <u>moo</u>. (Mrs. Kump)
A <u>mouse </u>likes to <u>squeak</u>. (Bob)
A <u>lion </u>likes to <u>roar</u>. (Laura)

### Theme:

This book could be an excellent foundational text for a unit on farms.

### Read-Aloud Books:

Nonfiction
- *A Day at Greenhill Farm* by Sue Nicholson (DK Publishing, 2001)
- *If It Weren't for Farmers* by Allan Fowler (Children's Press, 1993)

Fiction
- *Polar Bear, Polar Bear, What Do You Hear?* by Bill Martin, Jr. (Henry Holt and Co., Inc., 1991)
- *Cock-A-Doodle-Moo!* by Bernard Most (Harcourt, 1996)
- *Old Macdonald Had a Farm* illustrated by Pam Adams (Child's Play, 1989)
- *Barnyard Banter* by Denise Fleming (Henry Holt and Co., Inc., 1994)
- *The Farmer Didn't Wake Up* by Tamara Nunn (Creative Teaching Press, 1997) Only available as part of a classroom pack.

# Feathers for Lunch

## by Lois Ehlert
### (Harcourt Brace, 1990)

Look out! The cat is out and is hunting for something new for lunch. The many colorful birds appear to be tasty possibilities. However, birds can fly and cats cannot. So, for this cat, it's . . . "feathers for lunch." Once again, Lois Ehlert's bright, cheerful illustrations delightfully enhance the rhyming text.

### Purpose:
Build background knowledge and read for enjoyment.

**Before:**
- Cover Talk—Ask, "What do you notice? What is on the cat's nose? Why do you think it is there? Why do you think the author titled the book *Feathers for Lunch*?"

**During:**
- Reading and Thinking Aloud—Read the book, pausing occasionally to think aloud. Start on the title page and think aloud, "I wonder why the cat is looking at the bird? I guess I'll have to read to find out." Turn the page. Read the text. Say, "That looks like a cat tail. I wonder why the illustrator only shows the tail?" Turn the page. Read the text and then think aloud, "I wonder why the cat has such a strange face?" Read the text. Think aloud while turning the page, "I'm still not sure why the cat has such a strange face. I also wonder what the cat will eat for lunch?" Continue to read until the page with the illustration of the redheaded woodpecker has been read. Think aloud, "Now I know what the cat wants to eat. He wants to eat (pause)." Let the children complete the sentence with, "birds." Think aloud, "That's right, birds. I wonder if he gets to eat one. I hope not." Continue to read, stopping after the page with the illustration of a ruby-throated hummingbird. Think aloud while turning the page, "Those birds are really smart, they warn each other about the cat so they can fly away. I still wonder if the cat will catch any." Read to the end and think aloud, "That was silly, the cat only got (pause)!" Let the children complete the sentence with, "feathers for lunch."
- Shared Reading—Invite the students to join in and share the reading of the story.

**After:**
- Following Up—Follow up on one of the Cover Talk questions: "Why do you think the author titled this book *Feathers for Lunch*?"

---

### Purpose:
Read the book again and review what happened in the story.

**Before:**
- Retelling—Allow students to retell the story during a picture walk.

**During:**
- Choral Reading—The whole class reads the text with you or you can assign parts to be read by different children.

**After:**
- Discussion—Talk about the story (**Who? What? Where? When? Why?**).

---

**Purpose:**
Identify the beginning, the middle, and the end of the story.
**Preparation/Materials Needed:**
- Beach Ball with questions
- Three sentence strips
- Pocket chart with header cards labeled: **Beginning, Middle, End.**

**Before:**
- Retelling—Allow children to retell the story during a picture walk.

**During:**
- Echo Reading—Read a line and let the children be your echo, repeating the line after you.

**After:**
- Discussion and Writing—Ask, "What happened at the beginning? In the middle? At the end?" Write student responses on sentence strips and place them in the pocket chart.
- Beach Ball Questions—Toss the beach ball. Assist the student who catches the ball in reading one of the questions. Allow students to answer the question. Encourage them to refer to the pocket chart or book cover when giving their answers.

---

**Purpose:**
Find the Rhymes and use spelling patterns to Make Words.
**Preparation/Materials Needed:**
- Highlighting tape
- Highlight the following words: **crack, back, munch, lunch.**
- Chart paper
- Letter vests or letters cards for the following rhyming pattern and beginning sounds: **-ack; t, r, p, b, l, c, s, m, n**
- Pocket chart from Day 3

**Before:**
- Restore Prior Experience—Mix up the sentence strips from Day 3 (above). Ask students to help you place them in the correct sequence.

**During:**
- Choral Reading—The whole class reads the text with you or you can assign parts to be read by different children.

**After:**
- Ask, "What did you notice today as we read the story? Which words were highlighted?" (rhyming pairs—crack/back and munch/lunch)
- Finding and Writing—Find the highlighted words, then write them on the chart paper. If needed, direct children to observe that there are pairs of words that rhyme using the same spelling pattern.
- Making Words the "Building-Blocks Way"—Pass out letter vests or cards for the spelling pattern **-ack**, as in **back**. Have the three children with **a, c,** and **k** stand together at the front of the room as you blend the sounds. Then, pass out cards for **t, r, p, b, l, c, s, m,** and **n**. Guide children with these cards to the front and have them stand with the -ack children to make new words. Be sure that **c + r, t + r, s + m,** and **b + l** get together at the front, then blend their sounds together and make more words.

---

**Purpose:**
Correctly label birds after listening to simple descriptions.
**Preparation/Materials Needed:**
- Large self-stick notes (3" x 6")
- Write the following bird names on large self-stick notes: **Blue Jay**, **Cardinal**, **Woodpecker**, **Hummingbird**, **Red-Winged Blackbird**, **Robin**.

**Before:**
- Playing *Can You Find Me?*—Give simple clues for the various birds in the big book. Have students locate an illustration of the bird in the big book. Place the appropriate self-stick note next to the bird illustration. (For example, for the blue jay: I am blue. Can you find me?)

**During:**
- Choral Reading—Assign groups and choral read in two parts, each group alternating the pages.

**After:**
- Drawing and Writing—Have each student draw one of the birds and write a sentence about it. Share the students' work and create a bulletin board or class book from their papers.

## Two-Day Format:

**Before:**
- Cover Talk (See Day 1, page 53.)

**During:**
- Reading and Thinking Aloud (See Day 1, page 53.)
- Shared Reading (See Day 1, page 53.)

**After:**
- Discussion and Writing (See Day 3, page 54.)

**Before:**
- Picture Walk (See Day 1, page 53.)

**During:**
- Choral Reading (See Day 5, above.)

**After:**
- Making Words the "Building-Blocks Way" (See Day 4, page 54.)
- Playing Can You Find Me? (See Day 5, above.)

**Predictable Chart Idea:**
The _____ had _____ for lunch.
The <u>monkey</u> had <u>bananas</u> for lunch. (Mrs. Birdsong)
The <u>tiger</u> had <u>apples</u> for lunch. (Robin)
The <u>bear</u> had <u>fish</u> for lunch. (Jay)

# Freight Train

## by Donald Crews
### (Mulberry, 1978)

Experience a trip aboard a freight train without ever leaving the classroom. This book introduces children to the types of train cars and color words.

### Purpose:
Build background knowledge and read for enjoyment.

**Before:**
- Cover Talk—Ask, "What do you notice?" Explain what a freight train is and how it differs from a passenger train. Ask, "Has anyone seen a freight train?"
- Building Background Knowledge and Making Connections—Create a web of the words related to trains (see example).

**During:**
- Read Aloud—Read the big book aloud to the students with full expression.
- Shared Reading—Invite the students to join in and share the reading of the story.

**After:**
- Discussion—Talk about the cars on a train and how they move together. Make a train of students and move around the room. Tell the class that when a student passes his desk, he must sit down.

---

### Purpose:
Use context, picture clues, and onset to Guess the Covered Word.

### Preparation/Materials Needed:
- Self-stick notes
- Index cards
- Pocket chart
- Place self-stick notes on the **color words** in the story.
- Write the color words on index cards and place them in the pocket chart.

**Before:**
- Retelling—Allow students to retell the story during a picture walk.

**During:**
- Choral Reading to Guess the Covered Word—The whole class reads the text with you or you can assign parts to be read by different children. Stop after each page. Ask, "Who thinks they can find the missing word in the pocket chart?" Make sure to have the student explain the strategy used to determine her choice. Reveal the covered word and reread the page.
- Echo Reading—Read a line and let the children be your echo, repeating the line after you.

**After:**
- Discussion—Talk about the colors of the cars on the freight train. Ask, "Which car or color was your favorite?"

### Purpose:

Highlight the names of train cars and talk about what the cars carry.

### Preparation/Materials Needed:

- Highlighting tape

**Before:**
- Retelling—Use the cover as a catalyst for retelling the story.

**During:**
- Echo Reading—Read a line and let the children be your echo, repeating the line after you. Be sure to have the children listen for the name of the cars on the train.
- Choral Reading and Highlighting—The whole class reads the text with you or you can assign parts to be read by different children. Stop after each two-page spread. Allow students to find and highlight the names of train cars. Make sure to talk with the students about how they located the word.

**After:**
- Discussion—Talk about all the cars on the train in the story. Ask, "What does each car carry?"

---

### Purpose:

Match train car names with the appropriate color words.

### Preparation/Materials Needed:

- Blank index cards
- Pocket chart
- Write the names of the train cars from the story on the blank index cards.
- Index cards of color words from Day 3 (above)
- Randomly place the index cards in a pocket chart.

**Before:**
- Matching the Color Words and Train Cars—Picture walk through the book, stopping at each two-page spread. Ask, "What train car is on this page?" Have a student locate the index card with the train name on it. Ask, "What color is the (train car name) on this page?" Have another student locate the index card with the color on it. Pair the train car card and color word card together in the pocket chart.

**During:**
- Choral Reading—The whole class reads the text with you or you can assign parts to be read by different children. Tell the children, "Let's read to see if we matched our colors and cars correctly."

**After:**
- Extending the Chart—Mix up the index cards and have students match them in the pocket chart. Use the book to check the pairings, if necessary.

---

### Purpose:

Participate in Doing the Book.

### Preparation/Materials Needed:

- Index cards and pocket chart from Day 4
- The "Props"—illustrations of the train cars
- Write the appropriate line of text from the page in the big book on the back of each train car illustration (for example, for the red caboose, write, "Red caboose at the back," for the orange tank, write "Orange tank car next," etc.)

**Before:**
- Reviewing—Mix up the index cards from Day 4 (above) and correctly pair them in the pocket chart.
- Presenting the Props—Discuss how to use the props in Doing the Book.
- Picture Walk—Determine the actions and their sequence for Doing the Book.

---

**During:**
- Doing the Book—Pass out the props. The class choral reads the text. The characters read their lines at the appropriate times, while moving around the room as part of a train. Repeat, allowing every child an opportunity to participate in the pantomime.

**After:**
- Discussion and Sequencing—Talk about the sequence of the cars in the train.

## Two-Day Format:

**Before:**
- Cover Talk (See Day 1, page 56.)
- Building Background Knowledge and Making Connections (See Day 1, page 56.)

**During:**
- Read Aloud (See Day 1, page 56.)
- Shared Reading (See Day 1, page 56.)

**After:**
- Discussion (See Day 3, page 57.)

**Before:**
- Picture Walk (See Day 1, page 56.)

**During:**
- Choral Reading (See Day 4, page 57.)

**After:**
- Doing the Book (See Day 5, page 57 and above.)
- Discussion and Sequencing (See Day 5, above.)

**Read-Aloud Books:**
- *Two Little Trains* by Margaret Wise Brown (HarperCollins Juvenile Books, 2001)
- *The Little Engine That Could* by Watty Piper (Grosset and Dunlap, 1978)
- *I Love Trains* by Philomen Sturges (HarperCollins Juvenile Books, 2001)
- *101 Cars on the Track* by Sam Wilson (Cartwheel Books, 2001)

# From Head to Toe

## by Eric Carle
### (Harcourt School, 1997)

Each page of this predictable book presents an animal that invites the reader to copy its body movements. Children will quickly want to wiggle, stomp, thump, and wave with each of the wonderfully illustrated animals.

**Purpose:**
Build background knowledge and read for enjoyment.

**Before:**
- Cover Talk—Ask, "What do you notice? What is the animal doing? Who wrote this book? Have we read any other books by Eric Carle?"
- Picture Walk—Start a discussion of each page with the question, "What do you notice?" Talk about the pictures and a few important words.

**During:**
- Read Aloud—Read the book aloud to the students with full expression. Allow the children to do the motions at the end of each page.
- Shared Reading—Invite students to join in and share the reading of the story.

**After:**
- Discussion—Talk about what each animal does in the story. As students return to their seats or move to another activity, have them act out what their favorite animal does in the story.

---

**Purpose:**
Highlight the names of animals.
**Preparation/Materials Needed:**
- Highlighting tape
- Chart paper

**Before:**
- Retelling—Allow students to retell the story during a picture walk.
- Reviewing—Ask, "What kinds of animals are in this story?" List the students' responses on the chart paper.

**During:**
- Echo Reading—Read a line and let the children be your echo, repeating the line after you.
- Choral Reading and Highlighting—The whole class reads the text with you or you can assign parts to be read by different children. Stop after each two-page spread. Allow students to find and highlight the names of animals. Make sure to talk with the students about how they located the words.

**After:**
- Checking the Chart—Use the highlighted words in the big book to check the chart. Add any names that were missing and cross off any names that were not in the big book.

---

## Purpose:
Highlight the names of body parts.
## Preparation/Materials Needed:
- Highlighting tape
- Chart paper
- Draw an outline of the human body on the piece of chart paper.

### Before:
- Retelling—Use the cover as a catalyst for retelling the story.

### During:
- Choral Reading and Highlighting—The whole class reads the text with you or you can assign parts to be read by different children. Stop after each two-page spread. Allow students to find and highlight the names of body parts. Make sure to talk with students about how they located the words.

### After:
- Discussion and Labeling—Talk about the body chart, then label the body parts using the highlighted words in the big book.

---

## Purpose:
Use context, picture clues, and beginning sounds to Guess the Covered Word.
## Preparation/Materials Needed:
- Self-stick notes
- Place self-stick notes on the following words: **sleep**, **wash**, **drink**, **eat**, **drive**.

### Before:
- Retelling—Use the cover as a catalyst for retelling the story.

### During:
- Choral Reading to Guess the Covered Word—Assign groups and choral read each page in two parts. One group read the animal's part. The other group reads the child's response. Take suggestions for the covered word, then uncover the beginning sound. Take additional suggestions if needed. Reveal the covered word, then reread the page. Take student suggestions for the covered word and read the sentence using each suggested word. Reveal the covered word and reread the page.

### After:
- Discussion—Talk about what happens in the story and pretend to sleep, wash, drink, eat and drive.

---

## Purpose:
Participate in Doing the Book.
## Preparation/Materials Needed:
- The "Props"—illustrations of animals in the story

### Before:
- Presenting the Props—Discuss how to use the props in Doing the Book.
- Picture Walk—Confirm the actions and their sequence for Doing the Book, making sure to talk about the pictures and important words.

### During:
- Doing the Book—Pass out the props. The class choral reads the text while the characters pantomime the actions. Repeat allowing every child an opportunity to participate in the pantomime.

### After:
- Discussion—Talk about the actions of the animals and which actions the children enjoyed most.

---

# Two-Day Format:

**Before:**
- Cover Talk and Picture Walk (See Day 1, page 59.)

**During:**
- Read Aloud (See Day 1, page 59.)
- Shared Reading (See Day 1, page 59.)

**After:**
- Discussion and Labeling (See Day 3, page 60.)

**Before:**
- Picture Walk (See Day 1, page 59.)

**During:**
- Choral Reading to Guess the Covered Word (See Day 4, page 60.)

**After:**
- Doing the Book (See Day 5, page 60.)

 **XTENSIONS**

**Predictable Chart Idea:**

I can _____ with my _____.
I can <u>write </u>with my <u>pencil</u>. (Mrs. Beignet)
I can <u>talk </u>with my <u>friend</u>. (Eve)
I can <u>play </u>with my <u>ball</u>. (Tom)

**Interactive Chart:**

An interactive chart can be made using the song, "If You're Happy and You Know It."

If you're happy and you know it shake your foot.
If you're happy and you know it shake your foot.
If you're happy and you know it,
Then, you really ought to show it.
If you're happy and you know it shake your foot.

**Read-Aloud Book:**
- *Clap Your Hands* by Lorinda Bryan Cauley (Paper Star, 1997)

# Growing Vegetable Soup

## by Lois Ehlert
### (Harcourt Brace, 1987)

Children are guided through the steps of making vegetable soup, from planting the vegetable seeds to cooking the soup. Each page is brilliantly illustrated with labeled pictures that enhance the text.

### Purpose:
Build background knowledge and read for enjoyment.

### Before:
- Cover Talk—Ask, "What do you notice? What is the title? Have you ever eaten vegetable soup? Why do you think the book is titled *Growing Vegetable Soup*?"
- Picture Walk—Start a discussion of each page with the question, "What do you notice?" Talk about the pictures and a few important words.

### During:
- Read Aloud—Read the big book aloud to the students with full expression.
- Shared Reading—Invite the students to join in and share the reading of the story.

### After:
- Discussion—Ask, "What vegetables can go into vegetable soup?" Write the responses on a web or a chart with the heading, **Vegetable Soup**.

---

### Purpose:
Use context, picture clues, and onset to Guess the Covered Word.

### Preparation/Materials Needed:
- Self-stick notes
- Place self-stick notes on the following words the first time they appear in the story: **soup, tools, seeds, plants, vegetables, wash, cook**.

### Before:
- Retelling—Allow students to retell the story during a picture walk.

### During:
- Choral Reading to Guess the Covered Word—The whole class reads the text with you. Stop after each page. Take suggestions for the covered word, then uncover the beginning sound. Take additional suggestions if needed. Reveal the covered word, then reread the page.

### After:
- Discussion—Write the five Ws (**Who? What? Where? When? Why?**) on the fingers of a white cotton gardening glove. Use the glove to guide the discussion of the story. Be sure to include vocabulary (covered words) as you talk about the story.

**Purpose:**
Talk about the types of jobs and highlight these jobs.
**Preparation/Materials Needed:**
- Highlighting tape
- Chart paper

**Before:**
- Retelling—Use the cover as a catalyst for retelling the story.

**During:**
- Echo Reading—Read a line and let the children be your echo, repeating the line after you.
- Choral Reading and Highlighting—The whole class reads the text with you or you can assign parts to be read by different children. Stop after each two-page spread. Allow students to find, highlight, and write any jobs that had to be done. Make sure to talk with the students about how they located the word.

**After:**
- Discussion—Talk about the jobs in this book. Ask, "Who did each job? Why?"

---

**Purpose:**
List the steps for growing vegetable soup.
**Preparation/Materials Needed:**
- Sentence strips
- Pocket chart

**Before:**
- Discussion and Writing—Ask, "How do you grow vegetable soup? What do you do first? Next? Last?" Write the suggestions on sentence strips. Discuss if the sentence strip should be placed in the beginning, middle, or end of the pocket chart. Finally, place the sentence strip in the pocket chart.

**During:**
- Choral Reading—The whole class reads the text with you or you can assign parts to be read by different children. Stop at the end of each two-page spread. Ask, "What happened on the page? Is this something we need to add to our chart?" Write any new steps on a sentence strip and add it to the pocket chart.

**After:**
- Discussion—Talk about the chart and what needs to be added and where to add it. Ask, "What do we need to do when growing vegetable soup?"

---

**Purpose:**
Make and eat vegetable soup.
**Preparation/Materials Needed:**
- Pots, bowls, utensils, etc.
- Hot plate (or make arrangements to cook the soup in the school kitchen)
- Use the recipe provided in the big book to buy the ingredients or have students bring the ingredients from home.
- Cut the vegetables in advance.
- Write the recipe on chart paper for all to see (optional).

**Before:**
- Predictions—Bring out the soup pot and ask, "Can you predict what we're going to use this pot for?"

**During:**
- Making the Vegetable Soup—As you read the recipe, refer to the ingredients list and directions to model reading for real life purposes.

**After:**
- Let's Eat! This might be a good day to invite parents and younger siblings.

## Two-Day Format:

**Before:**
- Cover Talk and Picture Walk (See Day 1, page 62.)

**During:**
- Read Aloud (See Day 1, page 62.)
- Shared Reading (See Day 1, page 62.)

**After:**
- Discussion (See Day 2, page 62.)

**Before:**
- Picture Walk (See Day 1, page 62.)

**During:**
- Echo Reading (See Day 3, page 63.)
- Choral Reading (See Day 4, page 63.)

**After:**
- Discussion and Writing (See Day 4, page 63.)

**Predictable Chart Idea:**
My garden will have _____.
My garden will have cauliflower. (Mr. Baldman)
My garden will have carrots. (Lindsey)
My garden will have green beans. (Marquis)

**Read-Aloud Books:**
- *Tops and Bottoms* by Janet Stevens (Harcourt Brace, 1995)
- *Stone Soup* by Marcia Brown (Scott Foresman, 1989)
- *Eating the Alphabet* by Lois Ehlert (Harcourt Brace 1989)
- *Vegetable Garden* by Douglas Florian (Voyager Books, 1996)
- *The Surprise Garden* by Zoe Hall (HarperCollins, 1998)

# I Like Me!

## by Nancy Carlson
### (Scholastic Big Books, 1988)

A delightful pig shares her positive attitude about herself and the things that she does.

**Purpose:**
Build background knowledge and read for enjoyment.

**Before:**
- Building Background Knowledge and Making Connections—Ask, "What do you like to do? What do you like best about yourself?"
- Cover Talk—Ask, "What do you notice?"

**During:**
- Read Aloud—Read the big book aloud to the students with full expression.
- Shared Reading—Invite the students to join in and share the reading of the story.

**After:**
- Discussion—Ask, "What did the pig like about herself?"

---

**Purpose:**
Reread the story and talk about the words the pig uses to describe herself.

**Preparation/Materials Needed:**
- Highlighting tape
- Highlight some of the words the pig uses to describe herself (**awesome**, **brave**, **kind**, etc.).

**Before:**
- Retelling—Allow the students to retell the story during a picture walk.

**During:**
- Choral Reading—The whole class reads the text with you or you can assign parts to be read by different children.

**After:**
- Discussion—Talk about the meanings and give examples of the target words (for example, "What does it mean to be **brave**? What does it mean to be **kind**? What kind of deed is the pig doing?").

**Purpose:**
Read to find out how the pig feels about herself.

**Before:**
- Retelling—Use the cover as a catalyst for retelling the story.

**During:**
- Choral Reading—The whole class reads the text with you or you can assign parts to be read by different children. Be sure to listen for how the pig describes herself.

**After:**
- Discussion—Talk about some of the important words and let children share some of their experiences. Ask, "Is anyone in this class brave? Kind?"
- Writing and Drawing—Have students write sentences about themselves and illustrate them (for example, "I am kind to my sister.").

---

**Purpose:**
Find and categorize character attributes.

**Preparation/Materials Needed:**
- Pocket chart with header cards labeled: **Fun Things to Do**, **Taking Care of Me**, **Parts of the Body**

**Before:**
- Retelling—Use the cover as a catalyst for retelling the story.

**During:**
- Choral Reading and Highlighting—The whole class reads the text with you, or you can assign parts to be read by different children. Stop after each two-page spread. Locate and write any information that will complete the chart.

**After:**
- Discussion—Talk about the words the pig uses to describe herself. Ask, "Why do you think this word belongs in this category?"

---

**Purpose:**
Find the problems and the solutions encountered by the main character.

**Preparation/Materials Needed:**
- Chart with the headings: **Problem** and **Solution**.
- Pocket chart from Day 4

**Before:**
- Reviewing—Mix up the attributes from the Day 4 pocket chart (above). Have students place the attributes in the appropriate columns.

**During:**
- Choral Reading—Assign groups and choral read in two parts, alternating the pages.
- Finding Problems and Solutions—Start at the page that says, "When I feel bad . . ." and reread the text, searching for problems and solutions. Write the problems and solutions on the chart.

**After:**
- Extending the Chart—Add other common childhood problems and their possible solutions (for example, Problem: Wanting something someone else has; Solution: Ask for it politely).

---

## Two-Day Format:

**Before:**
- Building Background Knowledge and Making Connections (See Day 1, page 65.)
- Cover Talk (See Day 1, page 65.)

**During:**
- Read Aloud (See Day 1, page 65.)
- Shared Reading (See Day 1, page 65.)

**After:**
- Discussion (See Day 2, page 65.)

**Before:**
- Picture Walk (See Day 1, page 65.)

**During:**
- Choral Reading (See Day 3, page 66.)

**After:**
- Finding Problems and Solutions (See Day 5, page 66.)

**Predictable Chart Idea:**

I like me! I _____.
I like me! I <u>can write great stories</u>. (Mrs. Smith)
I like me! I <u>like my picture</u>. (Eve)
I like me! I <u>like block parties</u>. (Delinda)

**Read-Aloud Books:**
- *ABC I Like Me!* by Nancy L. Carlson (Puffin, 1999)
- *Life Is Fun* by Nancy L. Carlson (Puffin, 1996)
- *How about a Hug?* by Nancy L. Carlson (Viking Children's Books, 2001)

# I Love Spiders

## by John Parker
### (Scholastic Big Books, 1988)

This book's main character has a strange affection for spiders. He loves them tall and small, old and bold, fat and flat. He just loves spiders because he is a spider.

**Purpose:**
Build background knowledge and read for enjoyment.

**Before:**
- Building Background Knowledge and Making Connections—Sing the song, "Itsy Bitsy Spider." Ask, "What do you think of when you see a spider? Why?"
- Cover Talk—Ask, "What do you notice? What is the title of the story? Why do you think someone might love spiders?"

**During:**
- Read Aloud—Read the big book aloud to the students with full expression.
- Shared Reading—Invite the students to join in and share the reading of the story. You may want to pause at the word spider and allow the students to provide the word.

**After:**
- Discussion—Ask the students, individually, "Do you like spiders?" Encourage the students to provide a reason with their responses.

---

**Purpose:**
Summarize what this story is all about, **spiders**.

**Preparation/Materials Needed:**
- Highlighting tape

**Before:**
- Retelling—Allow students to retell the story during a picture walk.
- Predictions—Predict how many times the word **spiders** will appear in the text.

**During:**
- Choral Reading and Highlighting—The whole class reads the text with you or you can assign parts to be read by different children. Stop after each two-page spread. Allow students to find and highlight the word, **spiders**.

**After:**
- Discussion—Talk about what the students learned from this book about spiders. Ask, "How many times was the word **spiders** used in this book? Why?" (It's all about spiders!) List students' responses on chart paper or the board.

**Purpose:**
Create a web for spiders
**Preparation/Materials Needed:**
- Chart paper
- Draw a web on chart paper.

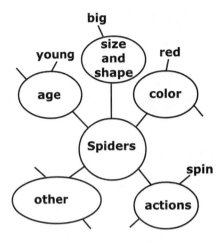

**Before:**
- Retelling—Use the cover as a catalyst for retelling the story.

**During:**
- Echo Reading—Read a line and let the children be your echo, repeating the line after you.
- Choral Reading and Finding Web Information—The whole class reads the text with you or you can assign parts to be read by different children. Stop after each two-page spread. Allow students to find information that can be added to the web.

**After:**
- Drawing and Writing—Draw a picture of a spider and complete the following sentence: I like my _____ spider because _____. Share the students' pictures and completed sentences and use them in a class book.

---

**Purpose:**
Discuss opposites found in this book.
**Preparation/Materials Needed:**
- Index cards
- Write the following words on index cards: **old, young, bold, shy, up, down, inside, outside, small, large.**

**Before:**
- Reviewing—Talk about opposites. Ask, "What are opposites?" Encourage students to give examples of opposites. "Let's read the book again and listen for opposites."

**During:**
- Choral Reading—Assign groups and choral read in two parts, alternating pages.

**After:**
- Discussion—Talk about the opposites found in the big book. Mix up the index cards and distribute them to the students. Have the students pair up with their opposites. Extend the activity by adding more pairs of opposites. Ask, "What other opposites do we know that are not found in the big book?"

---

**Purpose:**
Find rhyming words in the big book and use the spelling patterns to Make Words the "Building-Blocks Way."
**Preparation/Materials Needed:**
- Chart paper
- Letter vests or letters cards for the following rhyming pattern and beginning sounds: **-old; b, c, f, h, m, s, t**
- Highlighting tape

**Before:**
- Read Aloud—Pause as you read to highlight the following words: **small**, **all**, **old**, **bold**, **fat**, **flat**.

**During:**
- Choral Reading—The whole class reads the text with you or you can assign parts to be read by different children. Ask, "What did you notice today as we read the story? Which words were highlighted?" (rhyming words).
- Finding and Writing—Find the highlighted words, then write them in columns on the chart paper. If needed, direct children to observe that there are pairs of words that rhyme using the same spelling pattern (for example: sm<u>all</u>/<u>all</u>, <u>old</u>/b<u>old</u>, f<u>at</u>/fl<u>at</u>, etc.). Underline the spelling patterns.

**After:**
- Making Words the "Building-Blocks Way"—Pass out letter vests or cards for the spelling pattern **-old**, as in **bold**. Have the three children with **o**, **l**, and **d** stand together at the front of the room as you blend the sounds. Then, pass out cards for **b**, **c**, **f**, **h**, **m**, **s**, and **t**. Guide the children with these cards to the front and have them stand with the -old children to make new words using the spelling pattern and the other letter cards. Be sure that **s** + **c** get together at the front, then blend their sounds together and make more words.

# Two-Day Format:

**Before:**
- Building Background Knowledge and Making Connections (See Day 1, page 68.)
- Cover Talk (See Day 1, page 68.)

**During:**
- Read Aloud (See Day 1, page 68.)
- Shared Reading (See Day 1, page 68.)

**After:**
- Discussion (See Day 2, page 68.)

**Before:**
- Picture Walk (See Day 1, page 68.)

**During:**
- Echo Reading (See Day 3, page 69.)
- Choral Reading and Finding Web Information (See Day 3, page 69.)

**After:**
- Making Words the "Building-Blocks Way" (See Day 5, above.)

**Predictable Chart Ideas:**
Spiders _____.
Spiders <u>are big</u>. (Ms. Davis)
Spiders <u>are small</u>. (Virginia)
Spiders <u>have eight legs</u>. (John)
Spiders <u>are creepy</u>. (Paula)

# If the Dinosaurs Came Back

## by Bernard Most
### (Harcourt Brace, 1978)

Possible answers to the question, "What would happen if the dinosaurs came back?" are provided in a delightful and humorous manner.

**Purpose:**
Build background knowledge and read for enjoyment.

**Before:**
- Cover Talk—Ask, "What do you notice? What unusual thing is on the cover? What are dinosaurs doing in the city?"
- Predictions—Ask, "What do you think would happen if the dinosaurs came back?"

**During:**
- Read Aloud—Read the big book aloud to the students with full expression.
- Shared Reading—Invite the students to join in and share the reading of the story.

**After:**
- Discussion—Ask, "What would you do with a dinosaur?"

---

**Purpose:**
Read the book and discuss what was learned about **dinosaurs**.
**Preparation/Materials Needed:**
- Highlighting tape

**Before:**
- Retelling—Allow students to retell the story during a picture walk.
- Predictions—Predict how many times the word **dinosaur** will appear in the text.

**During:**
- Choral Reading and Highlighting—The whole class reads the text with you or you can assign parts to be read by different children. Stop after each two-page spread. Allow students to find, highlight, and tally the word **dinosaur**.

**After:**
- Discussion—Talk about why the word **dinosaur** appears so many times. Ask, "What did you learn about dinosaurs from this book?"

**Purpose:**
Use context, picture clues, beginning letter sounds, and memory to Guess the Covered Word.
**Preparation/Materials Needed:**
- Self-stick notes
- Place self-stick notes on the following words in the big book: **work**, **scare**, **build**, **stuck**, **teeth**, **love**.

**Before:**
- Retelling—Use the cover as a catalyst for retelling the story.

**During:**
- Choral Reading to Guess the Covered Word—The whole class reads the text with you or you can assign parts to be read by different children. Stop after each page and take suggestions for the covered word, then uncover the beginning sound. Take additional suggestions if needed. Reveal the covered word, then repeat the process for the other covered words.
- Echo Reading—Once all the covered words are revealed, echo read the text (read a line and let the children be your echo, repeating the line after you).

**After:**
- Discussion, Writing, and Drawing—Talk about the uncovered words and what they mean. Have students complete and illustrate the following sentence: "I learned that dinosaurs _____."

---

**Purpose:**
Highlight the words **could** and **would** and discuss what dinosaurs could and would do.
**Preparation/Materials Needed:**
- Highlighting tape

**Before:**
- Reviewing—Talk about all the things the class knows and has learned about dinosaurs.

**During:**
- Choral Reading and Highlighting—Assign groups and choral read in two parts. Stop after each two-page spread. Allow students to find and highlight the words, **could** and **would**.

**After:**
- Discussion—Talk about what dinosaurs **could** do and what students think dinosaurs **would** do if they lived today.

---

**Purpose:**
Find the names of dinosaurs in the story.
**Preparation/Materials Needed:**
- Highlighting tape

**Before:**
- Discussion—Talk about some of the dinosaurs in the story. List the dinosaurs on chart paper or the board. Tell the students, "Let's read to find out if we remembered all the dinosaurs."

**During:**
- Echo Reading—Read a line and let the children be your echo, repeating the line after you.

**After:**
- Writing and Drawing—Have students complete the sentence "One dinosaur I liked was _____," and add an illustration. Share the students' pictures and completed sentences and place them in a class book.

---

## Two-Day Format:

**Before:**
- Cover Talk and Predictions—(See Day 1, page 71.)

**During:**
- Read Aloud (See Day 1, page 71.)
- Shared Reading (See Day 1, page 71.)

**After:**
- Discussion (See Day 2, page 71.)

**Before:**
- Picture Walk (See Day 1, page 71.)

**During:**
- Choral Reading to Guess the Covered Word (See Day 3, page 72.)

**After:**
- Writing and Drawing (See Day 5, page 72.)

**Predictable Chart Ideas:**

What would happen if dinosaurs came back?
Dinosaurs could _____.
Dinosaurs could <u>clean my rain gutters</u>. (Miss Williams)
Dinosaurs could <u>raise the flag</u>. (Matt)
Dinosaurs could <u>pick apples</u>. (Elaine)

**Read-Aloud Books:**
- *Danny and the Dinosaur* by Syd Hoff (HarperCollins Juvenile Books, 1993)
- *Stanley* by Syd Hoff (HarperTrophy, 1992)
- *Whatever Happened to the Dinosaurs?* by Bernard Most (Voyager Books, 1987)
- *Dinosaur Cousins?* by Bernard Most (Voyager Books, 1990)

# If You Give a Mouse a Cookie

## by Laura Numeroff
### (HarperCollins Children's Books, 1996)

If you read this story to your class, they're going to ask you to read it again. If you read the story again, they'll probably want a cookie . . . and a glass of milk . . . and . . . .

**Purpose:**
Build background knowledge and read for enjoyment.

**Before:**
- Cover Talk—Ask, "What do you notice? What could happen in this story?"
- Picture Walk—Start a discussion of each page with the question, "What do you notice?" Model how to let the pictures help "figure out" words.

**During:**
- Read Aloud—Read the big book aloud to the students with full expression.
- Shared Reading—Invite the students to join in and share the reading of the story.

**After:**
- Discussion—Ask, "What are some of the things the mouse asked for?"

---

**Purpose:**
Review and read the story again.

**Before:**
- Retelling—Allow children to retell the story during a picture walk.

**During:**
- Choral Reading—The whole class reads the text with you or you can assign parts to be read by different children.

**After:**
- Discussion—Talk about what the children think might happen if they gave the mouse a cookie.
- Writing and Drawing—Have students complete the sentence "If I gave a mouse a cookie he would _____," and add an illustration.

**Purpose:**
Highlight and write the names of things the mouse might want or need.
**Preparation/Materials Needed:**
- Chart paper
- Highlighting tape

**Before:**
- Retelling—Use the cover as a catalyst for retelling the story.

**During:**
- Echo Reading—Read a line and let the children be your echo, repeating the line after you.
- Finding and Writing—The whole class reads the text with you or you can assign parts to be read by different children. Stop at the end of each two-page spread. Ask, "Is there anything the mouse might need on these pages?" Allow students to find and highlight the things the mouse might need. Make sure to talk with the students about how they located the information.

**After:**
- Listing—Write highlighted items on the chart while paging through the book. Talk about the chart with the students.

---

**Purpose:**
Complete simple cause and effect sentences.
**Preparation/Materials Needed:**
- Chart from Day 3
- Blank sentence strips
- Write the following sentence starters on sentence strips and place them in a pocket chart: If you give a mouse a cookie, . . . ; If you give a mouse some milk, . . . ; If you give a mouse a nail trimmer, . . . ; If you let a mouse trim his hair, . . . ; If you give a mouse a broom, . . . ; If you give a mouse a blanket and pillow, . . . ; If you give a mouse paper and crayons, . . . ; If you let a mouse draw a picture, . . . .

**Before:**
- Retelling—Retell the story using the information on the chart created on Day 3 (above).

**During:**
- Choral Reading—Assign groups and choral read in two parts, alternating sentences.

**After:**
- Completing Sentence Strips—Read the sentence starters in the pocket chart and write students' responses on new sentence strips.
- Reviewing—Mix up the beginning phrases and have students match the beginning phrases with the correct ending phrases.

---

**Purpose:**
Participate in Doing the Book.
**Preparation/Materials Needed:**
- The "Props"—illustrations of a mouse and all the items the mouse might need. (See the chart from Day 3, above.)
- Cookies and milk

**Before:**
- Presenting the Props—Discuss how to use them in Doing the Book.
- Picture Walk—Confirm the actions and their sequence for Doing the Book.

---

**During:**
- Doing the Book—Pass out the props. The class choral reads the text. The students with item cards will get up and stand by the "mouse" when their object is mentioned in the story. Repeat, allowing every child an opportunity to participate in the pantomime.

**After:**
- Drawing—Have students choose and draw their favorite scene from Doing the Book. The pictures can go home as souvenirs or be combined into a class book. Let the class enjoy a snack of cookies and milk while they complete their illustrations.

## Two-Day Format:

**Before:**
- Cover Talk and Picture Walk (See Day 1, page 74.)

**During:**
- Read Aloud (See Day 1, page 74.)
- Shared Reading (See Day 1, page 74.)

**After:**
- Listing (See Day 3, page 75.)

**Before:**
- Picture Walk (See Day 1, page 74.)

**During:**
- Echo Reading (See Day 3, page 75.)
- Choral Reading (See Day 4, page 75.)

**After:**
- Completing Sentence Strips (See Day 4, page 75.)

**Predictable Chart Idea:**

If you give a mouse _____, he will want _____.
If you give a mouse <u>an envelope</u>, he will want <u>a stamp</u>. (Ms. Zimmerman)
If you give a mouse <u>a piece of pizza</u>, he will want a<u> can of soda</u>. (Joan)
If you give a mouse <u>a baseball</u>, he will want <u>a baseball bat</u>. (Seth)

**Read-Aloud Books:**
- *If You Give a Moose a Muffin* by Laura Numeroff (Scott Foresman, 1991)
- *If You Take a Mouse to the Movies* by Laura Numeroff (HarperCollins Juvenile Books, 2000)
- *If You Give a Pig a Pancake* by Laura Numeroff (HarperCollins Juvenile Books, 1998)

# In a Dark, Dark Wood
# A Traditional Tale
## by Christine Ross
## (Wright Group, 1998)

This book retells this traditional tale that is often shared around campfires and at Halloween time. Children follow the text and illustrations from a dark, dark wood, to a dark, dark house, up dark, dark stairs, and finally to a dark, dark box containing a surprise.

**Purpose:**
   Build background knowledge and read for enjoyment.
**Preparation/Materials Needed:**
   • Chart paper

**Before:**
   • Cover Talk—Ask, "What do you notice?"
**During:**
   • Reading and Thinking Aloud—Pause after reading each two-page spread. Think aloud, "I wonder what will be in (or on) the (whatever is introduced)? (For example: I wonder what will be <u>in the dark, dark wood</u>?)
   • Shared Reading—Invite students to join in and share the reading of the story.
**After:**
   • Discussion—Talk about what was in the dark, dark wood. List student responses on chart paper or the board.

---

**Purpose:**
   Sequence what was found in the dark, dark wood.
**Preparation/Materials Needed:**
   • Sentence strips
   • Pocket chart
   • Dark colored marker (black or brown)

**Before:**
   • Retelling—Allow students to retell the story during a picture walk. Make sure they tell what was in the dark, dark wood.
**During:**
   • Choral Reading—The whole class reads the text with you or you can assign parts to be read by different children. Stop after each two-page spread. Using the dark marker, write what was seen on those pages (for example: in the wood, a house; in the house, the stairs; etc.).
**After:**
   • Discussion—Talk about what happened in the story, then read the sentence strips and put them in the pocket chart in the correct sequence.

---

### Purpose:
Use context, picture clues, and onset to Guess the Covered Word.

### Preparation/Materials Needed:
- Self-stick notes
- Index cards
- Place self-stick notes on the words that appear after the words, "dark, dark."
- Write the covered words on index cards. Place the index cards in the pocket chart.

### Before:
- Retelling—Use the cover as a catalyst for retelling the story.

### During:
- Choral Reading to Guess the Covered Word—The whole class reads the text with you. Stop after each page. Take suggestions for the covered word, then uncover the beginning sound. Take additional suggestions if needed. Reveal the covered word, then reread the page.

### After:
- Sequencing the Events—Mix up the index cards, then pass them out. Have the students with cards organize themselves in the story sequence. The remainder of the class choral reads the story to check the sequence.

---

### Purpose:
Create a new story by replacing the repeated adjective, **dark**.

### Preparation/Materials Needed:
- Chart paper
- Write the following story on the chart paper:

  In the _____, _____ wood, there was a _____, _____ house.
  In the _____, _____ house, there was a _____, _____ stair.
  In the _____, _____ stair, there was a _____, _____ room.
  In the _____, _____ room, there was a _____, _____ box.
  In the _____, _____ box, there was a _____ book!

### Before:
- Creating a New Story—Use student suggestions for filling in the blanks of the chart story. (Example: In a scary, scary wood, there was a spooky, spooky house.)

### During:
- Choral Reading—Assign groups and choral read the big book in two parts. One group reads the first part of the sentence ("In the dark, dark wood,"). The other group reads the second part of the sentence ("there was a . . . .").

### After:
- Discussion—Talk about how the new story is alike and different from the big book.

---

### Purpose:
Participate in Doing the Book.

### Before:
- Create pantomimes of the text for Doing the Book. Tell the student, "We are going on a walk in the dark, dark wood."
- Picture Walk to confirm the pantomimes and their sequence for Doing the Book.

**During:**
- Doing the Book—One group choral reads the text, while the other group pantomimes. Repeat and have the groups switch roles (the reading group pantomimes and the pantomime group reads).

**After:**
- Discussion—Talk about Doing the Book. Ask, "What was good about our play? What could have been better?"

## Two-Day Format:

**Before:**
- Cover Talk (See Day 1, page 77.)

**During:**
- Reading and Thinking Aloud (See Day 1, page 77.)
- Shared Reading (See Day 1, page 77.)

**After:**
- Discussion (See Day 1, page 77.)

**Before:**
- Picture Walk (See Day 1, page 77.)

**During:**
- Choral Reading to Guess the Covered Word (See Day 3, page 78.)

**After:**
- Creating a New Story (See Day 4, page 78.)

**Predictable Chart Idea:**

I saw a _____, in a dark, dark _____.
I saw a <u>raccoon</u>, in a dark, dark <u>garden</u>. (Mr. Crane)
I saw a <u>mouse</u>, in a dark, dark <u>basement</u>. (Ichabod)
I saw a <u>sea monster</u>, in a dark, dark <u>sea</u>. (Hawthorne)

**Read-Aloud Books:**
- *In the Haunted House* by Eve Bunting (Clarion Books, 1990)
- *Scary Party* by Sue Hendra (Candlewick Press, 1998)
- *In a Scary Old House* by Harriet Ziefert (Penguin USA, 1989)
- *In a Dark, Dark Room and Other Scary Stories* by Alvin Schwartz (HarperCollins Juvenile Books, 1984)
- *A Dark, Dark Tale* by Ruth Brown (Dial, 1991)

# In the Tall, Tall Grass

## by Denise Fleming
### (Henry Holt, 1993)

Denise Fleming's colorful illustrations make possible a trip through a grassland vibrant with life. The trip starts with a caterpillar munching his lunch and ends with looping and swooping bats in the middle of the night. The simple rhyming text is so entertaining that children will want to take the journey "in the tall, tall grass" again and again.

**Purpose:**
Build background knowledge and read for enjoyment.

**Before:**
- Cover Talk—Ask, "What do you notice? What do you think the boy is looking at? Where do you think the boy and the caterpillar are? What other animals might be seen in the tall, tall grass?"
- Picture Walk—Start a discussion of each page with the question, "What do you notice?"

**During:**
- Read Aloud—Read the big book aloud to the students with full expression.
- Shared Reading—Invite the students to join in and share the reading of the story.

**After:**
- Discussion—Talk about who or what was in the tall, tall grass. Dismiss students by having them individually complete the following sentence: In the tall, tall grass (name of student) saw a (selected student adds an animal name). (Example: In the tall, tall grass <u>Mary</u> saw a <u>bumblebee</u>.)

---

**Purpose:**
Highlight and write the names of animals.

**Preparation/Materials Needed:**
- Chart paper
- Highlighting tape

**Before:**
- Retelling—Allow students to retell the story during a picture walk.

**During:**
- Echo Reading—Read a line and let the children be your echo, repeating the line after you.
- Choral Reading and Highlighting—Choral read, stopping at the end of each two-page spread. Ask, "Are there any names of animals on these pages?" Allow students to find and highlight the names of animals. Make sure to talk with the students about how they located the information.

**After:**
- Web—Write highlighted items on a web while paging through the book (see example). Talk about the web when it is complete.

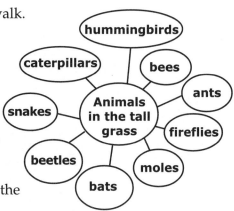

## Purpose:
Use context, picture clues, and memory to Guess the Covered Word.

## Preparation/Materials Needed:
- Self-stick notes
- Place self-stick notes on the word that follows each animal name (**lunch, sip, hum, flap, lug, glide, scratch, hurry, snap, flop, glow, swoop**).

**Before:**
- Retelling—Use the cover as a catalyst for retelling the story.

**During:**
- Choral Reading to Guess the Covered Word—The whole class reads the text with you or you can assign parts to be read by different children. Stop after each page. Take suggestions for the covered word, then uncover the beginning sound. Take additional suggestions if needed. Reveal the covered word, then reread the page.

**After:**
- Discussion—Talk about and list what was in the tall, tall grass.

---

## Purpose:
Find the rhyming words and use spelling patterns to Make Words.

## Preparation/Materials Needed:
- Chart paper
- Letter vests or letters cards for the following rhyming pattern and beginning sounds: **-ap; t, s, f, l, r, c, g, m, s, n**

**Before:**
- Retelling—Allow students to retell the story during a picture walk. Talk about the rhyming words in the text.

**During:**
- Choral Reading—The whole class reads the text with you or you can assign parts to be read by different children.

**After:**
- Rounding Up the Rhyming Words—Find the rhyming words and write them on the chart paper.
- Making Words the "Building-Blocks Way"—Pass out letter vests or cards for the spelling pattern **-ap**, as in **flap**. Have the two children with **a** and **p** stand together at the front of the room as you blend the sounds. Then, pass out cards for **t, s, f, l, r, c, g, m, s,** and **n**. Guide the children with these cards to the front and have them stand with the **-ap** children to make new words using the spelling pattern and the other letter cards. Be sure that **s + n, f + l, s + l, c + l,** and **s + t + r** get together at the front, then blend their sounds together and make more words.

---

## Purpose:
Participate in Doing the Book and discuss what happens in this story.

## Preparation/Materials Needed:
- The "Props"—two pictures of each animal in the book

**Before:**
- Presenting the Props—Discuss how to use the props in Doing the Book.
- Picture Walk—Confirm the actions and their sequence for Doing the Book.

**During:**
- Doing the Book—Pass out the props. The class choral reads the text while the characters pantomime the actions. Repeat, allowing every child an opportunity to participate in Doing the Book.

**After:**
- Discussion—Talk about what happened when the students were Doing the Book. Ask, "What did you do first? What happened next? What happened at the end?"

---

# Two-Day Format:

**Before:**
- Cover Talk and Picture Walk (See Day 1, page 80.)

**During:**
- Read Aloud (See Day 1, page 80.)
- Shared Reading (See Day 1, page 80.)

**After:**
- Discussion (See Day 3, page 81.)

**Before:**
- Picture Walk (See Day 1, page 80.)

**During:**
- Echo Reading (See Day 2, page 80.)
- Choral Reading to Guess the Covered Word (See Day 3, page 81.)

**After:**
- Making Words the "Building-Blocks Way" (See Day 4, page 81.)

**Predictable Chart Ideas:**

Near our school, I saw _____.
Near our school, I saw <u>many pretty flowers</u>. (Mrs. Nina Clock)
Near our school, I saw <u>red leaves</u>. (Pierre)
Near our school, I saw <u>a little dog</u>. (Korina)

In the big, big school, I saw _____.
In the big, big school, I saw <u>a tall principal</u>. (Mrs. Blockpart)
In the big, big school, I saw <u>a library</u>. (Delinda)
In the big, big school, I saw <u>boys and girls</u>. (Randy)

# It Begins with an A

## by Stephanie Calmenson
### (Scholastic Big Books, 1993)

Riddles written in rhyme introduce the letters of the alphabet. Each riddle's answer begins with the letter on the page. The illustrations provide obvious clues, allowing children to readily provide the answer.

**Purpose:**
Build background knowledge and read for enjoyment.

**Before:**
- Building Background Knowledge and Making Connections—Read one of the many alphabet books available.
- Cover Talk—Use the big book, not one of the alphabet books from the previous step. Ask, "What do you notice? Why do you think this book is titled *It Begins with an A*?"

**During:**
- Read Aloud—Read the big book aloud to the students with full expression.
- Shared Reading—Invite the students to join in and share the reading of the story.

**After:**
- Riddles—Have the children answer riddles about their classmates. For example: Who has on pink sneakers and has a name that begins with C? (Candy).

**Purpose:**
Use context, picture clues, and beginning letters to Guess the Covered Word.

**Preparation/Materials Needed:**
- Self-stick notes
- Place self-stick notes on six to eight important words in the text.

**Before:**
- Retelling—Allow children to retell the story during a picture walk.

**During:**
- Choral Reading to Guess the Covered Word—The whole class reads the text with you or you can assign parts to be read by different children. Read each page. Take suggestions for the covered word, then uncover the beginning sound. Take additional suggestions if needed. Reveal the covered word, then reread the page.

**After:**
- Riddles—Let the children make up their own riddles and tell them to partners.

## Purpose:

Find the answers to the riddles in the book.

## Preparation/Materials Needed:

- 26 half sheets of drawing paper, one for each letter of the alphabet
- Label each sheet of paper with one of the story's riddle answers: **airplane, ball, camera, doll, egg, foot, garage, hammer, icing, jar, kangaroo, lollipop, moon, nose, owl, pillow, quarter, rabbit, spaghetti, tail, umbrella, valentine, water, x-ray, yo-yo, zebra.**
- Place the riddle answers randomly in the pocket chart.

## Before:

- Retelling—Use the cover as a catalyst for retelling the story.

## During:

- Echo Reading—Read a line and let the children be your echo, repeating the line after you.
- Choral Reading and Finding—The whole class reads the text with you or you can assign parts to be read by different children. Stop after each page. Have a student find the riddle answer in the pocket chart. Let the student who locates the answer keep the paper to illustrate.

## After:

- Drawing—Have the students illustrate their riddles.
- Being a Book—Have students say their letters and words in alphabetical order. (For example: A is for airplane. B is for ball.)

---

## Purpose:

Review alphabetical order and beginning letter sounds.

## Preparation/Materials Needed:

- Students' riddle illustrations from Day 4

## Before:

- Review—Pass out the students' riddle illustrations from Day 3 (above). Have the students arrange themselves in alphabetical order. Sing the "ABC Song" slowly to check the students' work.

## During:

- Choral Reading—The whole class reads the text with you or you can assign parts to be read by different children. The student with the riddle answer should jump up and shout the answer at the appropriate time.

## After:

- Adding a Word—Select one riddle illustration at a time and have students make suggestions for other words beginning with the letter on the paper. Allow the student holding the picture to choose the word you will place on the back.
- Being a Book—Students say their letters and new words in alphabetical order. (For example: D is for dog. E is for eagle.)

---

## Purpose:

Create a souvenir of the big book.

## Preparation/Materials Needed:

- Students' riddle illustrations from Days 3 and 4 (above)
- Reproducible alphabet mini-book (available commercially or on the Internet at: http://www.enchantedlearning.com/letters/big/index.shtml)

---

**Before:**
- Reviewing—Pass out the drawings from Days 3 and 4 (page 84). Have students arrange themselves in alphabetical order. Do the Being a Book activity (see Day 4, page 84).
- Pass out copies of the reproducible mini-book.

**During:**
- Choral Reading—The whole class reads the reproducible mini-book with you or you can assign parts to be read by different children.

**After:**
- Souvenirs—Start coloring the pictures in the mini-book. Send the book home as a souvenir.

## Two-Day Format:

**Before:**
- Cover Talk (See Day 1, page 83.)

**During:**
- Read Aloud (See Day 1, page 83.)
- Shared Reading (See Day 1, page 83.)

**After:**
- Riddles (See Day 2, page 83.)

**Before:**
- Retelling (See Day 3, page 84.)

**During:**
- Choral Reading (See Day 4, page 84.)

**After:**
- Souvenirs (See Day 5, page 84 and above.)

**Predictable Chart Ideas:**

___ is for _____.
A is for <u>alligator</u>. (Ms. Packer)
B is for <u>boxes</u>. (Brett)
C is for <u>cheese</u>. (Baylee)

**Read-Aloud Books:**
- *Q is for Duck: An Alphabet Guessing Game* by Mary Elting and Michael Folsom (Houghton Mifflin Co., 1980)
- *Tomorrow's Alphabet* by George Shannon (Econo-Clad Books, 1999)
- *Dr. Seuss's ABC* by Dr. Seuss (Random House, 1963)

# It Looked Like Spilt Milk

## by Charles G. Shaw
### (HarperCollins, 1992)

It's a rabbit! It's a birthday cake! It's an angel! Or is it an ice-cream cone? A tree? Or just a bird? No, it's just a cloud in the sky!

**Purpose:**
Build background knowledge and read for enjoyment.

**Before:**
- Cover Talk—Ask, "What do you notice? What do you think this book is about? Why do you think the author used the title, *It Looked Like Spilt Milk*?"

**During:**
- Read Aloud—Read the big book aloud to the students with full expression.
- Shared Reading—Invite the students to join in and share the reading of the story.

**After:**
- Discussion—Talk about what objects the clouds looked like, then picture walk through the book with the class saying, "It looked like a (object on the page), but it wasn't."

---

**Purpose:**
Find and categorize the things the clouds looked like.

**Preparation/Materials Needed:**
- Index cards
- Highlighting tape
- Create four columns on a pocket chart using index cards with the following headings: **Animals**, **Foods**, **Plants**, **Other Things**.
- Pocket Chart

**Before:**
- Retelling—Allow children to retell the story during a picture walk.

**During:**
- Echo Reading—Read a line and let the children be your echo, repeating the line after you.
- Choral Reading, Highlighting, and Writing—The whole class reads the text with you or you can assign parts to be read by different children. Stop after each page. Ask, "What object did the cloud look like?" Allow students to find and highlight the word. Make sure to talk with the students about how they located the word, then write it on an index card.

**After:**
- Categorizing—Place the completed index cards in the correct column of the pocket chart.
- Extending the Chart—Mix up the index cards and have the students place them in the correct columns.

---

## Purpose:
Read the book again and focus on vocabulary words.
## Preparation/Materials Needed:
- Self-stick notes
- Place self-stick notes on the following vocabulary words: **rabbit, bird, ice-cream cone, flower, pig, birthday cake, sheep, great horned owl, squirrel, angel, cloud.**
- Write the same words on index cards, and place the index cards in the pocket chart.

### Before:
- Retelling—Use the cover as a catalyst for retelling the story.

### During:
- Choral Reading to Find the Missing Word—The whole class reads the text with you or you can assign parts to be read by different children. Stop at the end of each page. Ask, "Who thinks they can find the missing word in the pocket chart?" Make sure to have the student explain the strategy he used to determine his choice. Reveal the covered word and reread the page.

### After:
- Sentence Builders—Choose two or three sentences from the big book. "Build" each sentence by writing it on a sentence strip, then cutting the sentence apart, word by word. Give the words from one cut-up sentence to students who will go to the front of the room and "build" the sentence by arranging themselves in the right order. Repeat for each of your chosen sentences.

---

## Purpose:
Use spelling patterns to Make Words.
## Preparation/Materials Needed:
- Letter cards or letter vests for the following rhyming pattern and beginning sounds: **-ook; t, h, r, l, b, c**
- Chart paper
- Highlighting tape
- Highlight the following words on a single page in the big book: **it, like, but, looked.**

### Before:
- Discussion—Talk about the different things the clouds looked like in the book. Picture walk through the book and check the answers. Talk about the highlighted words.

### During:
- Choral Reading—Assign groups and choral read in two parts. One group reads the first sentence on each page. The other group reads the second sentence. Ask, "What did you notice today as we read the story? (Some of the words were highlighted.) Which words were highlighted?"

### After:
- Finding and Writing—Find the highlighted high-frequency words and write them on the chart paper. Be sure to focus on root words and endings. Ask, "What little word do you see in the word, looked? What letters are added to look to make looked?"
- Making Words the "Building-Blocks Way"—Pass out letter vests or cards for the spelling pattern **-ook**, as in **look**. Have the three children with **o, o,** and **k** stand together at the front of the room as you blend the sounds. Then, pass out cards for **t, h, r, l, b,** and **c**. Guide the children with these cards to the front and have them stand with the **-ook** children to make new words using the spelling pattern and the other letter cards. Be sure that **b + r** and **c + r** get together at the front, then blend their sounds together and make more words.

---

87 *Shared Reading with Big Books*

**Purpose:**
Participate in Doing the Book.
**Preparation/Materials Needed:**
- The "Props"—cards with pictures of the different cloud shapes presented in the book, along with the appropriate text from the book. Write the first sentence under the cloud shape and the second sentence on the other side of the card (for example, for the **flower** cloud write **It looked like a flower** under the picture and **But it wasn't a flower** on the opposite side).

**Before:**
- Presenting the Props—Discuss how to use the props in Doing the Book.
- Picture Walk—Confirm the actions and their sequence for Doing the Book.

**During:**
- Doing the Book—Pass out the cloud props. Students will read the text on the back of their cards at the appropriate time. The class responds by reading the text on the front of the cards. Repeat, allowing every child to use the props and participate in Doing the Book.

**After:**
- Drawing—Let the students draw clouds or make their own clouds using cotton balls. Have the children write and tell the class what they think their clouds look like.

## Two-Day Format:

**Before:**
- Cover Talk (See Day 1, page 86.)

**During:**
- Read Aloud (See Day 1, page 86.)
- Shared Reading (See Day 1, page 86.)

**After:**
- Discussion (See Day 1, page 86.)

**Before:**
- Picture Walk (See Day 1, page 86.)

**During:**
- Echo Reading (See Day 2, page 86.)
- Choral Reading (See Day 4, page 87.)

**After:**
- Doing the Book (See Day 5, above.)

## EXTENSIONS

**Read-Aloud Books:**
- *Little Cloud* by Eric Carle (Putnam Publishing Group, 1996)
- *The Cloud Book* by Tomie de Paola (Holiday House, Inc., 1986)
- *What Do You See in a Cloud?* by Allan Fowler (Children's Press, 1996)
- *Hi, Clouds* by Carol Greene (Children's Press, 1983)
- *Clouds* by Roy Wandelmaier (Troll Communications, 1990)

# Jeb's Barn

## by Andrea Butler
### (Celebration Press, 1995)

On Monday morning, everyone goes to help Jeb's family build a barn. Over seven hard days of work, the community raises a new barn for Jeb and his family.

**Purpose:**
   Build background knowledge and read for enjoyment.

**Before:**
   • Building Background Knowledge and Making Connections—Ask, "What does a builder have to do to make a house?"
   • Cover Talk—Ask, "What do you notice?" Link the building of a house to the story about building a barn. Include some information about the barn-raising efforts of Amish communities.
**During:**
   • Read Aloud—Read the big book aloud to the students with full expression.
   • Shared Reading—Invite the students to join in and share the reading of the story.
**After:**
   • Discussion—Ask, "What jobs have to be done to build a barn?"

---

**Purpose:**
   Use context, picture clues, and onset to Guess the Covered Word.
**Preparation/Materials Needed:**
   • Self-stick notes
   • Place self-stick notes on the following words in the big book: **frame**, **walls**, **roof**, **doors**, **shutters**.
   • Write the covered words on a second set of self-stick notes. Post these notes on the chalkboard.

**Before:**
   • Retelling—Allow students to retell the story during a picture walk. Talk about the pictures and remind the children to use the pictures to help them figure out difficult or unknown words.
**During:**
   • Choral Reading to Guess the Covered Word—The whole class reads the text with you. Stop after each page. Take suggestions for the covered word, then uncover the beginning sound. Take additional suggestions if needed. Reveal the covered word, then reread the page.
   • Echo Reading—Once all the words are uncovered, read a line and let the children be your echo, repeating the line after you.
**After:**
   • Discussion—Talk about the parts of the barn using the self-stick notes with the covered words written on them. Then, have students place the self-stick notes on the various parts of a picture of a barn. Finally, have the children draw a picture of a barn and label its parts.

---

**Purpose:**
List the highlighted days of the week.
**Preparation/Materials Needed:**
- Pocket chart
- Index cards
- Days of the week rhyme, chart, or poster
- Highlighting tape
- Highlight the **days of the week** in the big book.

**Before:**
- Retelling—Use the cover as a catalyst for retelling the story.

**During:**
- Echo Reading—Read a line and let the children be your echo, repeating the line after you.

**After:**
- Sequencing Game—Write each day of the week on an index card. Mix up the index cards. Pass them out to seven students. Allow the students to arrange themselves in the correct order. Use a days of the week rhyme, chart, or poster to help if needed. Repeat the game until all the students have had a chance to play.

---

**Purpose:**
Complete a cloze summary of the story.
**Preparation/Materials Needed:**
- Self-stick notes from Day 2
- Index cards from Day 3
- Chart paper
- Write the following on chart paper:
  On Monday everyone _____ to Jeb's farm at _____.
  On _____ they put up the _____ at _____.
  On _____ they put up the _____ at _____.
  On _____ they put on the _____ at _____.
  On _____ they put on the _____ and shutters at _____.
  On _____ they led the _____ into the barn at _____.
  On _____ they had a special _____ at _____.

**Before:**
- Reviewing—Match the self-stick notes from Day 2 (page 89) with the correct index cards from Day 3 (above). (For example: Tuesday - frame)

**During:**
- Choral Reading—Assign groups and choral read in two parts, alternating pages.

**After:**
- Completing the Chart—Talk with the children about how the barn was built, then complete the chart. Read the chart together.

**Purpose:**
Participate in Doing the Book.

**Before:**
- Actions—Create pantomimes of the text for Doing the Book.
- Picture Walk—Confirm the actions and their sequence for Doing the Book.

**During:**
- Doing the Book—One group reads the text together, while the other group pantomimes. Repeat, but have the children switch roles, allowing every child to participate in the pantomime.

**After:**
- Drawing—Have each student write a sentence about her favorite scene from Doing the Book, then illustrate the sentence. Assemble the student pictures into a class book.

# Two-Day Format:

**Before:**
- Building Background Knowledge and Making Connections (See Day 1, page 89.)
- Cover Talk (See Day 1, page 89.)

**During:**
- Read Aloud (See Day 1, page 89.)
- Shared Reading (See Day 1, page 89.)

**After:**
- Sequencing Game (See Day 3, page 90.)

**Before:**
- Picture Walk (See Day 1, page 89.)

**During:**
- Echo Reading (See Day 3, page 90.)
- Choral Reading to Guess the Covered Word (See Day 2, page 89.)

**After:**
- Drawing (See Day 5, above.)

**Read-Aloud Books:**
- *Building a House* by Byron Barton (William Morrow and Co., 1992)
- *How a House Is Built* by Gail Gibbons (Holiday House, Inc., 1996)
- *Building a House* by Annette Smith, Jenny Giles, and Beverley Randell (Rigby, 2001) Available only in six-packs.
- *Our New House* by Annette Smith, Jenny Giles, and Beverley Randell (Rigby, 2001) Available only in six-packs.
- *Bob the Builder* series (Simon Spotlight)

# The Jigaree

## by Joy Cowley
### (Wright Group, 1998)

What is a jigaree? He has wings and flies like a bee! Unlike you and unlike me, he has four legs on which to flee! What is a jigaree? He is a space creature created by Joy Cowley!

**Purpose:**
Build background knowledge and read for enjoyment.

**Before:**
- Building Background Knowledge and Making Connections—Ask, "What do you think a jigaree is?
- Cover Talk—Ask, "What do you notice? What object or creature do you think is a jigaree?"
- Picture Walk—Start a discussion of each page with the question, "What do you notice?" Focus on what the jigaree and the boy are doing. Remind students to use the pictures to help with any new or unknown words.

**During:**
- Read Aloud—Read the big book aloud to the students with full expression.
- Shared Reading—Invite the students to join in and share the reading of the story.

**After:**
- Discussion—Ask, "What is a jigaree? What does a jigaree do?"

---

**Purpose:**
Find the rhyming words in the big book and discuss jigarees.
**Preparation/Materials Needed:**
- Highlighting tape

**Before:**
- Retelling—Use the cover as a catalyst for retelling the story.

**During:**
- Echo Reading—Read a line and let the children be your echo, repeating the line after you.
- Choral Reading and Highlighting—The whole class reads the text with you or you can assign parts to be read by different children. Stop after each two-page spread. Allow students to find and highlight the rhyming words.

**After:**
- Discussion and Drawing—Ask students to complete the following sentence: A jigaree is _____. Then, have the students illustrate their completed sentences. The pictures can be sent home as souvenirs or assembled into a class book.

**Purpose:**
  Highlight and write all the words ending in **-ing**.
**Preparation/Materials Needed:**
  • Highlighting tape
  • Chart paper

**Before:**
  • Retelling—Use the cover as a catalyst for retelling the story.
**During:**
  • Choral Reading and Highlighting—Assign groups and choral read in two parts, alternating paragraphs. Stop after each two-page spread. Find and highlight any words that end with **-ing**.
**After:**
  • Listing—Write the highlighted words on the chart paper. Talk about the meanings of these words in the story.

---

**Purpose:**
  Find the root words for the words with the -ing ending.
**Preparation/Materials Needed:**
  • Chart from Day 3

**Before:**
  • Reviewing—Ask, "What things can a jigaree do?"
**During:**
  • Choral Reading—Assign groups and choral read in two parts, alternating paragraphs.
**After:**
  • Finding—Locate the Root Words in the story for the words on the chart from Day 3 (above). Write the root words next to the appropriate words on the chart.
  • Writing after Reading—Model how to create a simple story using the chart. (Example: I saw a jigaree jumping. A jigaree likes to jump.) Then, allow students to create their own sentences.

---

**Purpose:**
  Participate in Doing the Book.
**Preparation/Materials Needed:**
  • The "Props"—illustrations of a jigaree for half the class and illustrations of a boy in a space suit for half the class

**Before:**
  • Presenting the Props—Discuss how to use the props in Doing the Book.
  • Picture Walk—Confirm the actions and their sequence for Doing the Book.
**During:**
  • Doing the Book—Pass out the props. Children with the picture of the boy in a space suit read the first paragraph of each two-page spread while pantomiming. Children with the picture of the jigaree read the second paragraph of each two-page spread while pantomiming. Then, switch props and roles and Do the Book again.
**After:**
  • Discussion—Talk about Doing the Book. Ask, "Who made a good jigaree? Why?"

---

# Two-Day Format:

**Before:**
- Building Background Knowledge and Making Connections (See Day 1, page 92.)
- Cover Talk (See Day 1, page 92.)

**During:**
- Read Aloud (See Day 1, page 92.)
- Shared Reading (See Day 1, page 92.)

**After:**
- Discussion (See Day 1, page 92.)

**Before:**
- Picture Walk (See Day 1, page 92.)

**During:**
- Choral Reading (See Day 4, page 93.)

**After:**
- Reviewing (See Day 4, page 93.)

 **EXTENSIONS**

**Predictable Chart Idea:**
The jigaree is _____ me.
The jigaree is <u>running with</u> me. (Mrs. Worby)
The jigaree is <u>talking to</u> me. (Julie)
The jigaree is <u>playing with</u> me. (Travis)

**Interactive Chart Idea:**
Use the following rhyme pattern as a template to create new pages for the story.

I can see a jigaree. It is walking after me.

Walking here, walking there, jigarees walk everywhere.

**Read-Aloud Books:**
- Other *Jigaree* books by Joy Cowley (Wright Group)

# Jump, Frog, Jump!

## by Robert Kalan
### (Mulberry Books, 1995)

Danger lurks almost everywhere for the frog in this story. However, thanks to your students' warnings, he is sure to get away just in time. The frog manages to escape a hungry fish, a snake, a turtle, and even a net, but he needs to look out for the boys with a basket. Children will soon be chanting and jumping as they join you in reading this cumulative story.

**Purpose:**
>  Build background knowledge and read for enjoyment.

**Before:**
- Cover Talk—Ask, "What do you notice? What animals are in the drawing? What will happen in the story? Why do you think the story is titled *Jump, Frog, Jump*?"
- Picture Walk—Start a discussion of each page with the question, "What do you notice?" Pay careful attention to where the animals are and what they are doing on each page. Remind students to use the pictures to help with any new or unknown words.

**During:**
- Read Aloud—Read the big book aloud to the students with full expression.
- Shared Reading—Invite the students to join in and share the reading of the story.

**After:**
- Discussion—Talk about the story. Ask, "Why does the frog have to jump?"

---

**Purpose:**
>  Highlight the animal names.

**Preparation/Materials Needed:**
- Highlighting tape
- Two to three sentences from the big book written on sentence strips. Cut each sentence apart, place in a resealable plastic bag, and label the bag.

**Before:**
- Retelling—Allow students to retell the story during a picture walk. Ask, "What are some of the animals in our story?" Inform students that they will be searching for animal names while they read.

**During:**
- Echo Reading—Read a line and let the children be your echo, repeating the line after you.
- Choral Reading and Highlighting—The whole class reads the text with you or you can assign parts to be read by different children. Stop after each two-page spread. Allow students to find and highlight animal names.

**After:**
- Sentence Builders—Choose one sentence from the cut-up sentences. Give the words in one of the cut-up sentences to students who will go to the front of the room and "build" the sentence by arranging themselves in the right order. Let the students be "sentence builders" with the other cut-up sentences.

**Purpose:**
Create a chart of animals and their actions.
**Preparation/Materials Needed:**
- Chart paper
- Create a chart with the headings: **Animal** and **What did the animal do?**

**Before:**
- Reviewing—Ask, "What animals are in the story?" Write the responses in the **Animal** column of the chart.

**During:**
- Choral Reading—Assign groups and choral read in two parts. One group reads the repetitive text. The other group reads the remaining text.

**After:**
- Finding and Writing—Find the name of each animal and what actions it took, then write the actions on the chart (**What did the animal do?**).
- Sequencing—Work on sequencing the events in the story. Use numbers to indicate the sequence of events. Then, use the chart to retell the story.

---

**Purpose:**
Replace the repetitive text.
**Preparation/Materials Needed:**
- Self-stick notes or correction tape

**Before:**
- Retelling—Use the cover as a catalyst for retelling the story.

**During:**
- Choral Reading—Assign groups and choral read in two parts. One group reads the repetitive text. The other group reads the remaining text.

**After:**
- Replacing Words—Cover and replace each occurrence of the word, **jump**, using self-stick notes or correction tape (for example, <u>Leap</u>, frog, <u>leap</u>!)
- Choral Reading—The whole class reads the new text with you or you can assign parts to be read by different children.

---

**Purpose:**
Participate in Doing the Book.
**Preparation/Materials Needed:**
- The "Props"—Prepare pictures of the following characters: **fly, frog, fish, snake, turtle, net, kids, basket.** Write the characters' corresponding text from the book on the back of its picture (for example, on the back of the fly picture write, "the fly that climbed out of the water").

**Before:**
- Presenting the Props—Discuss how to use the props in Doing the Book.
- Picture Walk—Confirm the actions and their sequence for Doing the Book.

**During:**
- Doing the Book—Pass out the props. The children will need to sit in the proper sequence. Start by saying, "This is," and touch the first student's head. The student jumps up and says, "the fly that climbed out of the water." Say, "This is," and touch the second student. The second student says, "the frog that was under." The first student again says, "the fly that climbed out of the water." Then, the whole class says, "Who did the frog catch? The fly! Jump, Frog, Jump!" Continue in this fashion to the end of the story. Repeat, allowing every child an opportunity to participate.

**After:**
- Discussion—Talk about what happened in the big book. Ask, "What did the frog do? What did the turtle do?"

## Two-Day Format:

**Before:**
- Cover Talk and Picture Walk (See Day 1, page 95.)

**During:**
- Read Aloud (See Day 1, page 95.)
- Shared Reading (See Day 1, page 95.)

**After:**
- Finding and Writing/Sequencing (See Day 3, page 96.)

**Before:**
- Picture Walk (See Day 1, page 95.)

**During:**
- Echo Reading (See Day 2, page 95.)
- Choral Reading (See Day 3, page 96.)

**After:**
- Doing the Book (See Day 5, page 96 and above.)

**Predictable Chart Ideas:**
This is _____ who _____.
This is <u>Mrs. Reading</u>, who <u>said, "Good Morning" to Pat</u>.
This is <u>Pat</u>, who <u>shares a locker with Dottie</u>.
This is <u>Dottie</u>, who <u>let Lisa ride her bike</u>.

**Read-Aloud Books:**
Fiction
- *The Wide-Mouthed Frog: A Pop-Up Book* by Keith Faulkner (Dial Books for Young Readers, 1996)
- *Hop Jump* by Ellen Stoll Walsh (Voyager Books, 1993)
- *Frog and Toad* books by Arnold Lobel (HarperCollins)

Nonfiction
- *Tale of a Tadpole* by Karen Wallace (DK Publishing, 1998)

# The Little Red Hen

### retold by Brenda Parkes and Judith Smith
### (Rigby, 1984)

Little Red Hen finds a grain of wheat and endeavors to grow it, mill it, mix it, and bake it into bread. She hopes to enlist the help of her friends, but each one has better things to do. However, they all would like to help her eat the bread.

**Purpose:**
Build background and read for enjoyment.

**Before:**
- Cover Talk—Ask, "What do you notice? What is the hen doing? Can you find the word **little**? **Hen**? **Red**? It says, 'Retold by Brenda Parkes and Judith Smith.' What does this mean?"

**During:**
- Read Aloud—Read the big book aloud to the students with full expression. Stop before turning to last page and discuss if the Red Hen should let the others help eat the bread. Make sure to have the students give reasons for their responses.
- Shared Reading—Invite the students to join in and share the reading.

**After:**
- Discussion—Say, "The duck, the dog, the cat, and the pig all said they had better things to do when the red hen asked for help. What things could the animals have been doing that were more important then helping the hen?" (For example: The dog might have to dig a hole for his bone.)

---

**Purpose:**
Use context, picture clues, and onset to Guess the Covered Word.

**Preparation/Materials Needed:**
- Self-stick notes
- Place self-stick notes on the following words the first time they appear in the text: **wheat, plant, barked, meowed, grunted, home, bake, cooked, eat**.

**Before:**
- Retelling—Allow students to retell the story during a picture walk.

**During:**
- Choral Reading to Guess the Covered Word—The whole class reads the text with you. Stop after each page. Take suggestions for the covered word, then uncover the beginning sound. Take additional suggestions if needed. Reveal the covered word, then reread the page.

**After:**
- Discussion—Talk about who did all the work in the story. Ask, "Who should have helped? Why?" Write the five Ws (**Who? What? Where? When? Why?**) on the fingers of a white cotton gardening glove. Use the **story glove** to guide the discussion of the story. Be sure to include vocabulary (covered words) as you talk about the story.

**Purpose:**
Highlight the conversation between characters.
**Preparation/Materials Needed:**
- Highlighting tape (If possible, use two different tape colors; one for what Little Red Hen said, the other for what the remaining characters said.)

**Before:**
- Retelling—Use the cover as a catalyst for retelling the story.

**During:**
- Choral Reading—The whole class reads the text with you or you can assign parts to be read by different children.

**After:**
- Highlighting—Highlight what the characters say in the story. If possible, use two different tape colors; one for what Little Red Hen said, the other for what the remaining characters said.) Talk about the quotation marks.

---

**Purpose:**
List the steps Little Red Hen took to make bread.
**Preparation/Materials Needed:**
- Sentence strips
- Pocket chart

**Before:**
- Discussion and Writing—Ask, "What did the Little Red Hen have to do to make bread?" Write the suggestions on sentence strips. Discuss each sentence strip and whether it should be placed in the beginning, middle, or end of the pocket chart. Finally, place the sentence strip in the pocket chart. Tell the students, "Let's read the story one more time to see if we're right."

**During:**
- Choral Reading—Assign groups and choral read in three parts, stopping at the end of each two-page spread. Ask, "What happened on the page? Is this something we need to add to our chart?" Write any new steps on sentence strips and add them to the pocket chart.

**After:**
- Sequencing—Mix up the sentence strips and place them in correct order in the pocket chart.

---

**Purpose:**
Participate in Doing the Book.
**Preparation/Materials Needed:**
- The "Props"—pictures of a **cat**, **dog**, **pig**, **duck**, and **red hen**
- Ingredients for making bread from scratch or frozen bread dough
- Toaster oven or the oven in the school cafeteria

**Before:**
- Presenting the Props—Discuss how to use the props in Doing the Book.
- Picture Walk—Confirm the actions and their sequence for Doing the Book.

**During:**
- Doing the Book—Pass out the props. The class reads the narration. The children with the props add their dialogue at the appropriate times. Repeat the activity, allowing every child to use the props.

**After:**
- Discussion—Talk about what Little Red Hen needed to make bread and how she made bread.
- Snack—Make and bake bread from scratch or using frozen bread dough.

---

## Two-Day Format:

**Before:**
- Cover Talk (See Day 1, page 98.)

**During:**
- Read Aloud (See Day 1, page 98.)
- Shared Reading (See Day 1, page 98.)

**After:**
- Discussion and Writing (See Day 4, page 99.)

**Before:**
- Picture Walk (See Day 1, page 98.)

**During:**
- Choral Reading to Guess the Covered Word (See Day 2, page 98.)

**After:**
- Doing the Book (See Day 5, page 99.)

**Field Trip:**

Visit a bakery or doughnut shop.

**Read-Aloud Books:**
- *Little Red Hen (Makes a Pizza)* by Philemon Sturges (Dutton Books, 1999)
- *The Little Red Hen* by Byron Barton (HarperCollins Juvenile Books, 1997)
- *The Little Red Hen* by Paul Galdone (Houghton Mifflin Co., 1985)
- *The Little Red Hen* by Lucinda McQueen (Scholastic Big Books, 1993)

# Lunch

## by Denise Fleming
### (Harcourt Brace, 1992)

A very hungry mouse makes a lunch out of a variety of fruits and vegetables. Each two-page spread provides a brief description of the mouse's next menu item and includes a partial illustrated hint. Shouts of student predictions will be heard before turning each page.

**Purpose:**
  Build background and read for enjoyment.

**Before:**
- Building Background Knowledge and Making Connections—Ask, "What would you eat for lunch if you were very, very hungry?"
- Cover Talk—Ask, "What do you notice? What do you think a hungry mouse would like to eat for lunch?"

**During:**
- Read Aloud—Read the big book aloud to the students with full expression.
- Shared Reading—Invite the students to join in and share the reading.

**After:**
- Discussion—Ask, "What did the mouse eat for lunch?"

---

**Purpose:**
  Highlight the color words.
  **Preparation/Materials Needed:**
  - Highlighting tape

**Before:**
- Retelling—Allow students to retell the story during a picture walk.

**During:**
- Choral Reading and Highlighting—The whole class reads the text with you or you can assign parts to be read by different children. Stop after each page. Allow students to find and highlight the **color words**. Make sure to talk with the students about how they located the words.

**After:**
- Discussion—Talk about what the mouse ate for lunch and what color it was.
- Writing and Drawing—Have the students choose what they would eat if they were mice. Then, have them copy and complete the following sentence: If I were a mouse, I would eat _____. Finally, have the students draw what they would eat.

© Carson-Dellosa CD-2422    *Shared Reading with Big Books*

**Purpose:**
Highlight and categorize foods.

**Preparation/Materials Needed:**
- Highlighting tape
- Pocket chart
- Index cards
- Write the following categories on the index cards and place in the pocket chart: **Fruits**, **Vegetables**.

**Before:**
- Retelling—Use the cover as a catalyst for retelling the story.

**During:**
- Choral Reading and Highlighting —The whole class reads the text with you or you can assign parts to be read by different children. Stop after each two-page spread. Allow students to find and highlight the **foods**.

**After:**
- Writing and Categorizing—Write the highlighted foods on index cards and categorize them in the pocket chart.
- Reviewing—Mix up the index cards and place them in the appropriate columns in the pocket chart.

**Purpose:**
Write the descriptions of the fruits and vegetables.

**Preparation/Materials Needed:**
- Three-column chart labeled: **Describing Word, Color, Food**
- Pocket chart from Day 3

**Before:**
- Review—Mix up the index cards from Day 3 (above) and place them in the appropriate pocket chart columns.

**During:**
- Choral Reading—The whole class reads the text with you or you can assign parts to be read by different children. Stop after each two-page spread to find and write information that will complete the chart.

**After:**
- Retelling—Have the children retell the story using the chart.

**Purpose:**
Participate in Doing the Book and sequence the events from the big book.

**Preparation/Materials Needed:**
- Small samples of each fruit and vegetable mentioned in the big book. Be sure to have enough for each student in the class.
- Six pairs of mouse ears: Using gray construction paper, cut six strips of paper about two inches wide and long enough to wrap around a child's forehead (be sure to make each strip an inch or two longer so you can staple the ends together.) Cut out 12 large gray circles using a cup to trace a pattern. Cut out another smaller set of pink circles and glue or tape them inside the larger circles. Arrange two "ears" on each strip of paper and tape them in place. Once the ears are attached, tape the ends of the strip together to fit snuggly around a child's forehead.

 © Carson-Dellosa CD-2422

**Before:**
- Picture Walk through the big book to place the fruits and vegetables in the correct sequence.

**During:**
- Doing the Book—Pass out the mouse ears. The whole class reads the text with you or you can assign parts to be read by different children. The students with the mouse ears will do the mouse's actions at the table of samples. Repeat, allowing every child to be a mouse and eat the samples.

**After:**
- Discussion—Talk about what the mice ate first, next, and last.

## Two-Day Format:

**Before:**
- Building Background Knowledge and Making Connections (See Day 1, page 101.)
- Cover Talk (See Day 1, page 101.)

**During:**
- Read Aloud (See Day 1, page 101.)
- Shared Reading (See Day 1, page 101.)

**After:**
- Retelling (See Day 4, page 102.)

**Before:**
- Picture Walk (See Day 1, page 101.)

**During:**
- Choral Reading (See Day 4, page 102.)

**After:**
- Doing the Book (See Day 5, page 102.)
- Discussion (See Day 5, page 102.)

**Predictable Chart Ideas:**

A hungry mouse will eat _____.
A hungry mouse will eat a cookie. (Mrs. Frisby)
A hungry mouse will eat cheese. (Jonathan)
A hungry mouse will eat a hamburger. (Justin)

**Read-Aloud Books:**
- *Feathers for Lunch* by Lois Ehlert (Voyager Books, 1996)
- *The Very Hungry Caterpillar* by Eric Carle (Putnam Publishing Group, 1984)
- *The Little Mouse, the Red Ripe Strawberry, and the Big Hungry Bear* by Audrey Wood (Child's Play, 1998)

# Mary Had a Little Lamb

## by Sarah Josepha Hale
### (Scholastic Big Books, 1990)

The classic verse of a girl and her loyal lamb is brought to life with contemporary photographs.

**Purpose:**
Build background and read for enjoyment.

**Before:**
- Cover Talk—Ask, "What do you notice? What feelings do you think the girl has for the lamb? Why? What is the title of this book? What will happen in this story?"
- Picture Walk—The first few pages of the text will be familiar to many children. Allow them to read and track the text on these pages. Encourage predictions on the pages that contain the less familiar portions of the verse.

**During:**
- Read Aloud—Read the big book aloud to the students with full expression.
- Shared Reading—Invite the students to join in and share the reading.

**After:**
- Discussion—Talk about the story and the pictures. Ask, "Is this story real or make-believe?" Talk about where Mary went and the loyal lamb followed.

---

**Purpose:**
Highlight and tally each occurrence of the words, **Mary** and **lamb**.

**Preparation/Materials Needed:**
- Highlighting tape

**Before:**
- Retelling—Allow students to retell the story during a picture walk.

**During:**
- Choral Reading and Highlighting—The whole class reads the text with you or you can assign parts to be read by different children. Stop after each two-page spread. Allow students to find, highlight, and tally the words, **Mary** and **lamb**. Ask, "Who is this book all about?"

**After:**
- Discussion and Drawing—Talk to students about where they would go if they were Mary. Ask, "Could the lamb follow?" Have the students draw pictures of where they would go, being sure to put the lamb behind them.

**Purpose:**
Identify the beginning, the middle, and the end of the story.
**Preparation/Materials Needed:**
- Beach Ball with questions
- Three sentence strips
- Index cards
- Pocket chart
- Write the following headings on the index cards: **Beginning**, **Middle**, **End**. Place the headings in the pocket chart.

**Before:**
- Retelling—Use the cover as a catalyst for retelling the story.

**During:**
- Echo Reading—Read a line and let the children be your echo, repeating the line after you.

**After:**
- Discussion and Writing—Ask, "What happened at the beginning? In the middle? At the end?" Write the students' responses on sentence strips and place them in the appropriate columns on the pocket chart.
- Beach Ball Questions—Toss the beach ball. Assist the student who catches the ball in reading one of the questions. Allow students to answer the question. Encourage them to refer to the pocket chart or book cover when giving their answers.

**Purpose:**
Write and read photograph captions.
**Preparation/Materials Needed:**
- Large self-stick notes

**Before:**
- Reviewing—Sing the song, "Mary Had a Little Lamb."

**During:**
- Choral Reading—The whole class reads the text with you or you can assign parts to be read by different children. Stop after each two-page spread and talk about the pictures on those pages.

**After:**
- Photograph Captions—Write captions for the large full-page photographs in the big book on the large self-stick notes.
- Choral Reading—Assign groups and choral read in two parts. One group reads the text. The other group reads the added captions.

**Purpose:**
Participate in Doing the Book.
**Preparation/Materials Needed:**
- The "Props"—pictures of Mary and the little lamb

**Before:**
- Presenting the Props—Discuss how to use the props in Doing the Book.
- Picture Walk—Confirm the actions and their sequence for Doing the Book.

**During:**
- Doing the Book—Pass out the props. The class reads the text together while the characters pantomime the actions. Repeat the activity allowing every child an opportunity to participate in the pantomime.

**After:**
- Discussion—Write the five W's (**Who? What? Where? When? Why?**) on the fingers of a white cotton gardening glove. Use the glove to guide the discussion of the story.

## Two-Day Format:

**Before:**
- Cover Talk and Picture Walk (See Day 1, page 104.)

**During:**
- Read Aloud (See Day 1, page 104.)
- Shared Reading (See Day 1, page 104.)

**After:**
- Discussion and Writing (See Day 3, page 105)

**Before:**
- Picture Walk (See Day 1, page 104.)
- Discussion (See Day 1, page 104.)

**During:**
- Echo Reading (See Day 3, page 105)
- Choral Reading (See Day 4, page 105.)

**After:**
- Photograph Captions (See Day 4, page 105.)

**Predictable Chart Ideas:**
Mary had a little lamb. Its fleece was as white as snow.
One day the lamb followed Mary to _____.
The lamb followed Mary to <u>the museum</u>. (Mrs. Law)
The lamb followed Mary to <u>the zoo</u>. (Cecilia)
The lamb followed Mary to <u>the store</u>. (Carol)

**Interactive Chart Idea:**
Create new verses for "Mary Had a Little Lamb."

# Meanies

## by Joy Cowley
### (Wright Group, 1998)

The Meanies are friendly, ogre-like creatures that like to do some of the strangest things. The repetitive text and delightful illustrations will cause children to laugh and groan at the many disgusting things Meanies do, such as sleeping in garbage cans or eating old bubble gum.

**Purpose:**
Build background and read for enjoyment.

**Before:**
- Cover Talk—Ask, "What do you notice? What do you think the silly creatures are called? What other books have we read by this author?"
- Picture Walk—Start a discussion of each page with the question, "What do you notice?"

**During:**
- Read Aloud—Read the big book aloud to the students with full expression.
- Shared Reading—Invite the students to join in and share the reading.

**After:**
- Discussion—Ask, "Do you like Meanies? Why or why not?"

---

**Purpose:**
Review the story and work on vocabulary using context, picture clues, and memory to Guess the Covered Word.

**Preparation/Materials Needed:**
- Self-stick notes
- Place self-stick notes on the following words in the big book: **sleep**, **wash**, **drink**, **eat**, **drive**, **do**.

**Before:**
- Retelling—Allow children to retell the story during a picture walk.

**During:**
- Choral Reading to Guess the Covered Word—The whole class reads the text with you or you can assign parts to be read by different children. Stop after each page. Take suggestions for the covered word, then uncover the beginning sound. Take additional suggestions if needed. Reveal the covered word, then reread the page.

**After:**
- Discussion—Talk about Meanies. Ask, "Are Meanies real?" Be sure to include the new vocabulary words (**sleep**, **wash**, **drink**, **eat**, **drive**, **do**) in your discussion.

**Purpose:**
Create a chart of describing how Meanies do things and summarize the book.
**Preparation/Materials Needed:**
- Chart paper
- Use the chart paper to make a chart with the headings: **Action** and **What do Meanies do?**

**Before:**
- Reviewing—Ask, "What did the Meanies do in the story?" Write the students' responses on the chart.

**During:**
- Choral Reading—Assign groups and choral read in two parts. One group reads questions. The other group reads the responses.
- Finding and Writing—Find the information needed to complete the chart (actions and what the Meanies do).

**After:**
- Reviewing—Use the chart to write a summary of the story with your students.

---

**Purpose:**
Extend the story by describing what Meanies should do.
**Preparation/Materials Needed:**
- Large self-stick notes or correction tape
- Chart from Day 3

**Before:**
- Reviewing—Use the chart from Day 3 (above) to make sentences that summarize the story. After each sentence, discuss what Meanies should do (for example, Meanies should sleep in beds.)

**During:**
- Choral Reading—Assign groups and choral read in two parts. One group reads the questions. The other group reads the responses.

**After:**
- Adding Text—At the end of each page, add a new phrase that describes what Meanies should do. Write the new phrase on a self-stick note and add it to the page. For example, after, "That's where Meanies sleep," add, "but they should sleep in beds."

---

**Purpose:**
Participate in Doing the Book.
**Preparation/Materials Needed:**
- Paper and crayons for illustrating

**Before:**
- Reviewing—Assign groups and choral read in two parts. One groups reads the questions. The other group reads the responses. Both groups read the parts added by the class. Talk about students' favorite parts of the story.

**During:**
- Doing the Book—Group students with others who liked the same thing about the Meanies. The whole class reads the questions. The groups read their responses (what they liked about the Meanies).

---

**After:**

- Drawing and Writing—Have the students complete the following sentence: I like when the Meanies _____. Then, have the students illustrate their favorite parts of the story. The students' illustrations may be sent home as souvenirs of the big book. Encourage the students to discuss the illustration and the story with their parents.

## Two-Day Format:

**Before:**

- Cover Talk and Picture Walk—(See Day 1, page 107.)

**During:**

- Read Aloud (See Day 1, page 107.)
- Shared Reading (See Day 1, page 107.)

**After:**

- Discussion (See Day 2, page 107.)

**Before:**

- Picture Walk (See Day 1, page 107.)

**During:**

- Choral Reading (See Day 3, page 108.)

**After:**

- Drawing and Writing (See Day 5, above.)

### Read-Aloud Books:

- Other *Meanies* books by Joy Cowley (Wright Group)
- *Where the Wild Things Are* by Maurice Sendak (HarperTrophy, 1988)
- *Glad Monster, Sad Monster: A Book About Feelings* by Ed Emberly and Susan Miranda (Little, Brown and Co., 1997)

# Monster Sandwich

## by Joy Cowley
### (Wright Group, 1989)

What kind of sandwich will a monster eat? Joy Cowley suggests that a monster would eat a lettuce, cheese, pickle, meat, tomato, and mud sandwich. GROSS . . . but children love it!

**Purpose:**
Build background and read for enjoyment.

**Before:**
- Cover Talk—Ask, "What do you notice? Can you make any predictions after seeing this cover and hearing the title?"
- Picture Walk—Start a discussion of each page with the question, "What do you notice?"

**During:**
- Read Aloud—Read the big book aloud to the students with full expression.
- Shared Reading—Invite the students to join in and share the reading.

**After:**
- Discussion—Ask, "What do you want on your sandwich?" Each student responds in a complete sentence and returns to her seat.

---

**Purpose:**
Highlight the names of food.

**Preparation/Materials Needed:**
- Highlighting tape

**Before:**
- Retelling—Allow students to retell the story during a picture walk.

**During:**
- Echo Reading—Read a line and let the children be your echo, repeating the line after you.
- Choral Reading and Highlighting—The whole class reads the text with you or you can assign parts to be read by different children. Stop after each page. Allow students to find and highlight the names of food. Make sure to talk with the students about how they located the words.

**After:**
- Discussion—Talk about the book. Have the students draw a picture of a monster sandwich.

### Purpose:
Use context, picture clues, and onset to Guess the Covered Word.

### Preparation/Materials Needed:
- Self-stick notes
- Index cards
- Pocket Chart
- Place self-stick notes on the following words in the big book: **lettuce, cheese, pickles, meat, tomatoes, mud, bread**.
- Write the covered words on index cards and place them in the pocket chart.

### Before:
- Retelling—Allow students to retell the story during a picture walk.

### During:
- Choral Reading—The whole class reads the text with you or you can assign parts to be read by different children. Stop after each page and ask, "Who thinks they can find the missing word in the pocket chart?" Make sure to have the student explain the strategy used to determine his choice. Take other suggestions for the covered word, then uncover the beginning sound. Reveal the covered word, then reread the page.

### After:
- Sequencing—Mix up the index cards and have students place them in the order they are added to the sandwich.

---

### Purpose:
List the steps needed to make a "monster sandwich."

### Preparation/Materials Needed:
- Sentence strips
- Pocket chart

### Before:
- Discussion and Writing—Ask, "What do you need to do to make a monster sandwich?" Write the students' suggestions on sentence strips. Discuss each sentence strip and whether it should be placed in the beginning, the middle, or the end of the pocket chart. Finally, place the sentence strip in the pocket chart. When all the sentence strips are in the pocket chart, tell the students, "Let's read the story one more time to see if we're right."

### During:
- Choral Reading—The whole class reads the text with you or you can assign parts to be read by different children. Stop after each page and ask, "What happened on this page? Is this something we need to add to our chart?" Write any new steps on sentence strips and add them to the pocket chart.

### After:
- Sequencing—Mix up the sentence strips and have students place them in the correct order in the pocket chart.

**Purpose:**
Participate in Doing the Book.
**Preparation/Materials Needed:**
- All the ingredients to make a monster sandwich: lettuce, cheese, pickles, meat, tomatoes, chocolate frosting (mud), and bread.
- Plastic knives
- Self-stick notes
- Write the following words on self-stick notes: **lettuce**, **cheese**, **pickles**, **meat**, **tomatoes**, **mud**.

**Before:**
- Labeling the Illustrations—Have the students move the self-stick notes to the correct illustrations. Make sure the student explains the strategy used to select the correct self-stick note.

**During:**
- Choral Reading—The whole class reads the text with you.

**After:**
- Making Monster Sandwiches—Model for the students how to make a monster sandwich. Then, let each student make her own monster sandwich.
- Drawing and Writing—Each student draws a picture and writes about his favorite monster sandwich. The picture can be sent home as a souvenir or placed in a class book.
- Let's Eat!

## Two-Day Format:

**Before:**
- Cover Talk (See Day 1, page 110.)
**During:**
- Read Aloud (See Day 1, page 110.)
- Shared Reading (See Day 1, page 110.)
**After:**
- Discussion (See Day 1, page 110)

**Before:**
- Discussion and Writing (See Day 4, page 111.)
**During:**
- Choral Reading (See Day 4, page 111.)
**After:**
- Making Monster Sandwiches (See Day 5, above.)

**Predictable Chart Idea:**
I want _____ on my sandwich.
I want <u>onions</u> on my sandwich. (Mr. Hallytosis)
I want <u>pizza sauce</u> on my sandwich. (Marie)
I want <u>cheese</u> on my sandwich. (Tyler)

# Mouse Paint

## by Ellen Stoll Walsh
### (Harcourt Brace, 1989)

What can happen when three white mice see three jars of paint—red, blue, and yellow? The curious furry creatures jump in the jars and find out. The results are orange, green, and purple feet. At the same time, children are cleverly introduced to the concepts of primary and secondary colors.

**Purpose:**
Build background and read for enjoyment.
**Preparation/Materials Needed:**
• Red, yellow, and blue tempera paints

**Before:**
• Cover Talk—Ask, "What do you notice? Why do you think the mice are painting? What do you think will happen in this book?"

**During:**
• Reading and Thinking Aloud—At the first two-page spread, think aloud, "I wonder if the cat will catch the mice?" Read the text and say, "Oh, good! The cat can't find them." Turn the page, read the text, and think aloud, "What will those mice do with the paint?" Turn the page, read the text, and think aloud, "I remember getting paint on my feet once. I made a terrible mess." Turn the page, read the text, and think aloud, "Now what are they going to do? I hope they clean up that mess." Turn the page and think aloud, "Look, they're not cleaning up. What are they doing?" Continue reading to the end of the story.
• Shared Reading—Invite the students to join in and share the reading.

**After:**
• Discussion—Talk about mixing colors and show the class how this is done by having students mix tempera paint colors.

---

**Purpose:**
Highlight the color words.
**Preparation/Materials Needed:**
• Highlighting tape

**Before:**
• Retelling—Allow students to retell the story during a picture walk.

**During:**
• Echo Reading and Highlighting—Read a line and let the children be your echo, repeating the line after you. Stop after each page. Allow students to find and highlight the color words. Make sure to talk with the students about how they located the words.

**After:**
• Writing and Drawing—Have the children write the three color words (**red**, **blue**, **yellow**) on a sheet of paper. Below each color word, have the students draw pictures of things that are that color (for example, under **red**, students might draw a tomato).

### Purpose:
Review the story and discuss the action words (verbs) in the big book.
### Preparation/Materials Needed:
- Self-stick notes
- Place self-stick notes on the following words the first time they appear in the story: **climbed, dripped, stepped, stirred, hopped, mixed, splashed, shouted, washed.**

### Before:
- Retelling—Use the cover as a catalyst for retelling the story.
### During:
- Choral Reading to Guess the Covered Word—The whole class reads the text with you or you can assign parts to be read by different children. Stop after each page. Take suggestions for the covered word, then uncover the beginning sound. Take additional suggestions if needed. Reveal the covered word, then reread the page.
### After:
- Discussion—Talk about the covered words. Use waxed string (available from school supply stores) to underline the root words. Have the children "act out" the verbs climbed, dripped, stepped, etc.

### Purpose:
Discuss primary colors and mixing colors.
### Preparation/Materials Needed:
- Index cards
- Pocket chart
- Write the following words on index cards: **red, blue, yellow, purple, green, orange.**

### Before:
- Discussion—Talk about the primary colors and what colors you get when you mix two primary colors.
### During:
- Choral Reading—Assign groups and choral read in two parts, alternating pages.
### After:
- Creating Sentences—Create sentence about mixing colors by placing the index cards with the color words in a pocket chart. For example: Red and yellow make orange.

### Purpose:
Make a souvenir book.
### Preparation/Materials Needed:
- Make enough copies of the *Mouse Colors* book pattern on page 167 for your entire class.

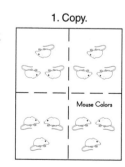

**Before:**
- Read Aloud—Read the text of the souvenir book

**During:**
- Coloring—Let students color the pictures on the pages of the souvenir book. Model for students how to fold the page together to form a book.

**After:**
- Souvenirs—Send the souvenir book home.

2. Fold.   3. Send home.

# Two-Day Format:

**Before:**
- Cover Talk (See Day 1, page 113.)

**During:**
- Reading and Thinking Aloud (See Day 1, page 113.)
- Shared Reading (See Day 1, page 113.)

**After:**
- Writing and Drawing (See Day 2, page 113.)

**Before:**
- Picture Walk (See Day 1, page 113.)

**During:**
- Choral Reading to Guess the Covered Word (See Day 3, page 114.)

**After:**
- Creating Sentences (See Day 4, page 114.)
- Souvenir Books (See Day 5, page 114 and above.)

**Predictable Chart Idea:**
My _____ is _____.
My tiger is orange. (Ms. Taft)
My house is yellow. (Keri)
My cat is black. (Jason)

---

# Mud Walk

## by Joy Cowley
### (Wright Group, 2000)

No collection of predictable book titles would be complete without Joy Cowley's famous Mrs. Wishy-Washy. In this book the cow, the pig, and the duck are once again neck deep in mud. In fact, they are stuck! The three mud-lovers get out with the help of Mrs. Wishy-Washy, who, of course, insists they take a bath.

**Purpose:**
Build background and read for enjoyment.

**Before:**
- Building Background Knowledge and Making Connections—Read *Mrs. Wish-Washy* by Joy Cowley (Wright Group, 1998). Ask, "What animals are in the book? Why do you think the animals jumped in the mud? What did Mrs. Wishy-Washy make the animals do? Why?"
- Cover Talk—Talk about the cover of *Mud Walk*. Ask, "What do you notice? What could happen in this story?"

**During:**
- Read Aloud—Read the big book *Mud Walk* aloud to the students with full expression.
- Shared Reading—Invite the students to join in and share the reading.

**After:**
- Discussion—Talk about the story with your students. Then, touch the shoulders of your students, one at a time. When you touch a shoulder, the student should say, "Oh lovely mud!" You should add, "said (student's name)." Then, that student goes to her seat.

---

**Purpose:**
Identify the beginning, the middle, and the end of the story.

**Preparation/Materials Needed:**
- Beach Ball with questions
- Three sentence strips
- Three index cards
- Pocket chart
- Create headings for the pocket chart by writing each of the following words on a separate index card: **Beginning**, **Middle**, **End**. Place the completed cards in the pocket chart.

**Before:**
- Retelling—Allow children to retell the story during a picture walk.

**During:**
- Echo Reading—Read a line and let the children be your echo, repeating the line after you.

**After:**
- Discussion and Writing—Ask, "What happened at the beginning? In the middle? At the end?" Write the students' responses on the sentence strips and place them in the pocket chart.
- Beach Ball Questions—Toss the beach ball. Assist the student who catches the ball in reading one of the questions. Allow students to answer the question. Encourage them to refer to the pocket chart or book cover when giving their answers.

**Purpose:**
Create a chart of animals, their sounds, and the noise they made in the mud.

**Preparation/Materials Needed:**
- Highlighting tape
- Chart paper
- Use the chart paper to make a three-column chart with the headings: **Animal Name**, **Animal Sound**, and **Mud Sound**.

**Before:**
- Reviewing—Ask, "What animals are in *Mud Walk*?" List student responses in the Animal Name column.

**During:**
- Choral Reading and Highlighting—The whole class reads the text with you or you can assign parts to be read by different children. Stop at the end of each page and highlight the name of each animal, the sound it made, and the sound it made in the mud.

**After:**
- Completing the Chart—Write the highlighted words (pages 8-11 in the big book) on the chart.
- Extending the Chart—Add other animals and their sounds to the chart. Discuss what possible sound each animal could make in the mud.

**Purpose:**
Use spelling patterns to Make Words.

**Preparation/Materials Needed:**
- Chart paper
- Letter vests or letters cards for the following rhyming pattern and beginning sounds: **-ip**; **t, n, f, l, r, d, h, k, s**

**Before:**
- Reviewing—Review the story using the chart made on Day 3 (above).

**During:**
- Choral Reading—The whole class reads the text with you or you can assign parts to be read by different children.

**After:**
- Finding Sound Words—Say, "Let's find the words for the sounds the animals made in the mud. We will use some of those sound words to Make Words."
- Making Words the "Building-Blocks Way"—Pass out letter vests or cards for the spelling pattern **-ip**, as in **drip**. Have the two children with **i** and **p** stand together at the front of the room as you blend the sounds. Then, pass out cards for **t, n, f, l, r, d, h, k,** and **s**. Guide the children with these cards to the front and have them stand with the **-ip** children to make new words using the spelling pattern and the other letter cards. Be sure that **f + l, s + l,** and **s + k** get together at the front, then blend their sounds together and make more words.

**Purpose:**
Participate in Doing the Book.

**Preparation/Materials Needed:**
- The "Props"—pictures of **Mrs. Wishy-Washy, duck, cow,** and **pig**
- Hotel-size bars of soap or pictures of a wash tub to color

**Before:**
- Presenting the Props—Discuss how to use the props in Doing the Book.
- Picture Walk—Confirm the actions and their sequence for Doing the Book.

**During:**
- Doing the Book—Pass out the props. The class reads the text together while the characters pantomime the actions. Repeat, allowing every child to participate in the pantomime.

**After:**
- Souvenirs—Pass out hotel-size bars of soap or a picture of a wash tub for the children to cut out and color. Discuss what children will tell their parents about the souvenir and the book they read during the past week.

---

# Two-Day Format:

**Before:**
- Building Background Knowledge and Making Connections (See Day 1, page 116.)
- Cover Talk (See Day 1, page 116.)

**During:**
- Read Aloud (See Day 1, page 116.)
- Shared Reading (See Day 1, page 116.)

**After:**
- Discussion and Writing (See Day 2, page 116.)

**Before:**
- Picture Walk (See Day 1, page 116.)

**During:**
- Choral Reading (See Day 4, page 117.)
- Echo Reading (See Day 2, page 116.)

**After:**
- Doing the Book (See Day 5, page 117 and above.)
- Souvenirs (See Day 5, above.)

**Predictable Chart Idea:**
"Oh lovely mud!" said the _____.
"Oh lovely mud!" said the <u>chicken</u>. (Ms. Farmer)
"Oh lovely mud!" said the <u>cat</u>. (Marquis)
"Oh lovely mud!" said the <u>sheep</u>. (Jacqueline)

Conclude the Predictable Chart with:

"In the tub you go!" said Mrs. Wishy-Washy.
"Wishy-washy, wishy-washy!"
"Wishy-washy, wishy-washy!"

**Read-Aloud Books:**
- Other *Mrs. Wishy-Washy* books by Joy Cowley (Wright Group)

# The Napping House

## by Audrey Wood
### (Harcourt Brace, 1984)

It is a rainy day and everyone is napping. The mouse is slumbering. The cat is snoozing. The dog is dozing. The child is dreaming, and granny is snoring. And everyone is on top of the other! That is, until a flea comes and bites the mouse at the top of the pile. Soon the nap is over for everyone, even the sun.

**Purpose:**
Build background knowledge and read for enjoyment.

**Before:**
- Building Background Knowledge and Making Connections—Tell the students about a time when you had to share a bed and were unable to get much sleep. Allow students to share their own experiences.
- Cover Talk and Picture Walk—Ask, "What do you notice about the cover?" Start a discussion of each page with the question, "What do you notice?" Talk about some important words using pictures.

**During:**
- Read Aloud—Read the big book aloud to the students with full expression.
- Shared Reading—Invite the students to join in and share the reading.

**After:**
- Discussion—Talk about the story. Then, have the students pretend to be napping on the floor. You are the flea. The students jump up and go to their seats when bitten (touched softly) by the flea.

---

**Purpose:**
Highlight the names of the story characters.

**Preparation/Materials Needed:**
- Highlighting tape

**Before:**
- Retelling—Allow children to retell the story during a picture walk.

**During:**
- Echo Reading—Read a line and let the children be your echo, repeating the line after you.
- Choral Reading and Highlighting—The whole class reads the text with you or you can assign parts to be read by different children. Stop after each two-page spread. Allow students to find and highlight the names of any story characters. Make sure to talk with the students about how they located the names.

**After:**
- Discussion—Talk about the story using the five Ws (**Who? What? Where? When? Why?**). Use a story glove (see page 98) if possible. Be sure to talk about the characters as children answer the questions.

### Purpose:
Identify the beginning, the middle, and the end of the story.

### Preparation/Materials Needed:
- Beach Ball with questions
- Three sentence strips
- Three index cards
- Pocket chart
- Create headings for the pocket chart by writing each of the following words on a separate index card: **Beginning, Middle, End**. Place the completed cards in the pocket chart.

### Before:
- Retelling—Use the cover as a catalyst for retelling the story.

### During:
- Echo Reading—Read a line and let the children be your echo, repeating the line after you.

### After:
- Discussion and Writing—Ask, "What happened at the beginning? In the middle? At the end?" Write the students' responses on sentence strips and place them in the pocket chart.
- Beach Ball Questions—Toss the beach ball. Assist the students in reading a question on the ball. Allow students to answer the question. Encourage them to refer to the pocket chart or book cover when giving their answers.

### Purpose:
To reread the story and discuss new vocabulary words.

### Preparation/Materials Needed:
- Highlighting tape
- Place highlighting tape on the following words: **sleeping, snoring, dreaming, dozing, slumbering, bites, scares, claws, thumps, bumps, breaks**.

### Before:
- Retelling—Use the cover as a catalyst for retelling the story.

### During:
- Choral Reading—The whole class reads the text with you or you can assign parts to be read by different children.

### After:
- Reviewing—Talk about the highlighted words on each page. Ask, "Which highlighted words end with **-ing**? Which highlighted words are plural? What letter do the plural words have added at the end?"

### Purpose:
Participate in Doing the Book.

### Preparation/Materials Needed:
- The "Props"—pictures of a **granny**, a **child**, a **dog**, a **cat**, a **mouse**, and a **flea**

### Before:
- Presenting the Props—Discuss how to use the props in Doing the Book.
- Picture Walk—Confirm the actions and their sequence for Doing the Book.

**During:**
- Doing the Book—Pass out the props. The class choral reads the text while the characters pantomime the actions. Repeat the activity, allowing every child to participate in the pantomime.

**After:**
- Discussion—Talk about each character in the story and tell what they did in the story.

## Two-Day Format:

**Before:**
- Building Background Knowledge and Making Connections (See Day 1, page 119.)
- Cover Talk and Picture Walk (See Day 1, page 119.)

**During:**
- Read Aloud (See Day 1, page 119.)
- Shared Reading (See Day 1, page 119.)

**After:**
- Discussion and Writing (See Day 3, page 120.)

**Before:**
- Picture Walk (See Day 1, page 119.)

**During:**
- Echo Reading (See Day 3, page 120.)
- Choral Reading (See Day 4, page 120.)

**After:**
- Doing the Book (See Day 5, page 120 and above.)
- Discussion (See Day 5, above.)

**Predictable Chart Idea:**
I wake up when _____.
I wake up when <u>the alarm clock rings</u>. (Ms. Fayette)
I wake up when <u>the train whistle blows</u>. (Jeff)
I wake up when <u>the dog barks</u>. (Shirley)

# Oh No!

## by Bronwen Scarffe
### (Mondo, 1994)

Oh No! There is a hole in this book from front to back! In fact, there are fifteen different holes. Children will delight in the dilemma each page presents, since they have had first-hand experiences with holes.

## Purpose:
Build background and read for enjoyment.

### Before:
- Cover Talk—Ask, "What do you notice? Have you ever had a hole in something?"

### During:
- Read Aloud—Read the big book aloud to the students with full expression.
- Shared Reading—Invite the students to join in and share the reading.

### After:
- Discussion—Ask, "Can you think of some holes at school? At home?"

---

## Purpose:
Reread the story and discuss new vocabulary words.

### Preparation/Materials Needed:
- Self-stick notes
- Place self-stick notes on the following words in the big book: **sock, shoe, umbrella, sweater, skirt, tooth, beach ball, kite, teddy bear, school bag, glove, hat, apple, pear, pie.**

### Before:
- Retelling—Allow students to retell the story during a picture walk.

### During:
- Choral Reading to Guess the Covered Word—The whole class reads the text with you or you can assign parts to be read by different children. Stop after each page. Take suggestions for the covered word, then uncover the beginning sound. Take additional suggestions if needed. Reveal the covered word, then reread the page. Talk about how the pictures can help you with these words.

### After:
- Discussion—Talk about all the things that had holes (Oh no!). Read the text, stopping occasionally at an important word which the students should read. Point to the picture to reinforce using them as word clues.

**Purpose:**
Create a chart of things with holes and how to fix the holes.
**Preparation/Materials Needed:**
- Chart paper
- Using the chart paper, create a chart with the headings: **Things with Holes** and **How to Fix the Holes**.

**Before:**
- Reviewing—Ask, "What things had holes in the story?" List student responses on the chart.

**During:**
- Choral Read—The whole class reads the text with you or you can assign parts to be read by different children.

**After:**
- Finding and Writing—Find the things with holes in the big book, then write them on the chart under **Things with Holes**.
- Discussion—Talk about and write ways to fix the holes. If a solution cannot be found, mark the object with a question mark.

---

**Purpose:**
Categorize the object words.
**Preparation/Materials Needed:**
- Chart paper
- Use the chart paper to create a four-column chart with the following headings: **Clothes, Food, Toys, Other Things**.

**Before:**
- Retelling—Use the cover as catalyst for retelling the story.

**During:**
- Choral Reading and Highlighting—The whole class reads the text with you or you can assign parts to be read by different children. Stop at the end of each page. Find the things with holes and highlight them.

**After:**
- Completing the Chart—Write the highlighted words in the correct column on the chart.
- Discussion—Talk about the number of things that had holes (Oh no!). Ask, "How many things in this story had holes?" Count the items during a picture walk to check your answers.

---

**Purpose:**
Participate in Doing the Book.
**Preparation/Materials Needed:**
- The "Props"—Gather the following items or pictures of the following items: **sock, shoe, umbrella, sweater, skirt, tooth, beach ball, kite, teddy bear, school bag, glove, hat, apple, pear, pie**.
- Place colored circular stickers (holes) on all the items or the pictures.

**Before:**
- Presenting the Props—Discuss how to use the props in Doing the Book.
- Picture Walk—Confirm the actions and their sequence for Doing the Book.

---

**During:**
- Doing the Book—Pass out the props. Students with props pantomime the actions as the rest of the class choral reads the text. Repeat, allowing every child to participate in the pantomime.

**After:**
- Souvenirs—Give each student a circular sticker ("hole") to place on his clothing. Encourage the students to discuss the sticker and story with their parents.

# Two-Day Format:

**Before:**
- Cover Talk (See Day 1, page 122.)

**During:**
- Read Aloud (See Day 1, page 122.)
- Shared Reading (See Day 1, page 122.)

**After:**
- Discussion (See Day 2, page 122.)

**Before:**
- Picture Walk (See Day 1, page 122.)

**During:**
- Choral Reading and Highlighting (See Day 4, page 123.)

**After:**
- Discussion (See Day 3, page 123.)
- Doing the Book (See Day 5, page 123 and above.)

**Predictable Chart Ideas:**
I had a hole in my _____.
I had a hole in my <u>bike tire</u>. (Mr. Bikealot)
I had a hole in my <u>basketball</u>. (Mike)
I had a hole in my <u>backyard</u>. (Mary)

**Read-Aloud Books:**
- *The Real Hole* by Beverly Cleary (Econo-Clad Books, 1999)
- *Color Farm* by Lois Ehlert (HarperCollins Children's Books, 1999)
- *Color Zoo* by Lois Ehlert (HarperCollins Children's Books, 1999)

# Peanut Butter and Jelly
## A Play Rhyme
### by Nadine Bernard Westcott
### (Dutton, 1992)

Two children create an enormous peanut butter and jelly sandwich from scratch with a little help from a baker, a few elephants, and some household pets.

**Purpose:**
Build background knowledge and read for enjoyment.

**Before:**
- Building Background Knowledge and Making Connections—Discuss making a peanut butter and jelly sandwich.
- Cover Talk—Ask, "What do you notice?" Make sure the students discuss the size of the bread and the use of the saw to cut the bread.

**During:**
- Read Aloud—Read the big book aloud to the students with full expression.
- Shared Reading—Invite the students to join in and share the reading.

**After:**
- Discussion—Talk about all the silly things in the pictures.

**Purpose:**
Reread the story and discuss new vocabulary words.

**Preparation/Materials Needed:**
- Self-stick notes
- Index cards
- Pocket chart
- Place self-stick notes on the following words the first time they appear in the story: **bake, slice, crack, mash, spread, smear, peanuts, dough, grapes**.
- Write the covered words on index cards, then place them in the pocket chart.

**Before:**
- Retelling—Allow students to retell the story during a picture walk.

**During:**
- Choral Reading to Find the Missing Word—The whole class reads the text with you or you can assign parts to be read by different children. Stop after each page. Ask, "Who thinks they can find the missing word in the pocket chart?" Make sure to have the students explain the strategies they used to determine their choices. Reveal the missing word and reread the page.

**After:**
- Discussion—Talk about how they made peanut butter and jelly sandwiches in the big book.

## Purpose:
List the steps for making a peanut butter and jelly sandwich.
### Preparation/Materials Needed:
- Sentence strips
- Pocket chart

**Before:**
- Discussion and Writing—Ask, "How do you make a peanut butter and jelly sandwich?" Write each suggestion on a sentence strip. Discuss if the sentence strip should be placed in the beginning, the middle, or the end of the pocket chart. Finally, place the sentence strip in the pocket chart.

**During:**
- Choral Reading—The whole class reads the text with you or you can assign parts to be read by different children. Stop at the end of each two-page spread. Ask, "What happened on these pages? Is this something we need to add to our chart?" Write any new steps on sentence strips and add them to the pocket chart.

**After:**
- Review—Check to see that the sentences in the pocket chart are in the correct sequence, then read the chart together.

---

## Purpose:
Participate in Doing the Book.
### Preparation/Materials Needed:
- Suggested actions are listed on the final page of the big book.

**Before:**
- Actions—Talk about the actions each character in the story will use when Doing the Book. Use the illustrations as a catalyst for creating actions for each page.

**During:**
- Doing the Book—Divide the class into two groups. While one group reads the text, the other group performs the pantomime actions. Repeat the activity, allowing every child to participate in the pantomime.

**After:**
- Writing and Drawing—Let each student complete the following sentence: My favorite sandwich is a _____. Then, let the students illustrate their sentences. Assemble the completed pages and make a class book.

---

## Purpose:
Make and eat peanut butter and jelly sandwiches.
### Preparation/Materials Needed:
- Bread, peanut butter, jelly
- Plastic knives
- Sentence strips
- Pocket chart

**Before:**
- Reviewing—Ask, "What do we need to do to make a peanut butter and jelly sandwich?" Write the directions from the students' responses and post them in the pocket chart.

**During:**
- Modeling—Show the class how to make a peanut butter and jelly sandwich. Make sure to refer to the directions posted in the pocket chart. Let students read the directions and make sandwiches.

**After:**
- Let's eat!

---

  © Carson-Dellosa CD-2422

# Two-Day Format:

**Before:**
- Cover Talk (See Day 1, page 125.)

**During:**
- Read Aloud (See Day 1, page 125.)
- Shared Reading (See Day 1, page 125.)

**After:**
- Doing the Book (See Day 4, page 126.)

**Before:**
- Picture Walk (See Day 1, page 125.)

**During:**
- Choral Reading to Find the Missing Word (See Day 2, page 125.)

**After:**
- Discussion and Writing (See Day 3, page 126.)
- Modeling/Let's Eat (See Day 5, page 126.)

**Read-Aloud Book:**
- *Teddy Bear, Teddy Bear* illustrated by Michael Hague (William Morrow and Co., 1993)

**Internet Resources:**

http://www.gameskidsplay.net/jump_rope_ryhmes/index.htm

http://www.cs.uwf.edu/~skulikow/jrope3/jumprope.htm

http://www-personal.umich.edu/~pfa/dreamhouse/nursery/rhymes/

# The Pig that Learned to Jig

## by Alan Trussell-Cullen
### (Wright Group, 1993)

A pig learns how to do a jig with the help of his barnyard friends.

**Purpose:**
Build background and read for enjoyment.

**Before:**
- Cover Talk—Ask, "What do you notice? What is the pig doing? The book title is *The Pig that Learned to Jig*. What do you think a jig is?"
- Picture Walk—Start a discussion of each page with the question, "What do you notice?"

**During:**
- Read Aloud—Read the big book aloud to the students with full expression.
- Shared Reading—Invite the students to join in and share the reading.

**After:**
- Discussion—Ask, "What would you do to help the pig learn to jig?"

---

**Purpose:**
Reread the story and discuss the animal names used in the book.

**Preparation/Materials Needed:**
- Self-stick notes
- Index cards
- Pocket chart
- Place self-stick notes on the **names of animals** the first time they appear in the story.
- Write the animal names on index cards. Place the index cards in the pocket chart.

**Before:**
- Retelling—Allow students to retell the story during a picture walk.

**During:**
- Choral Reading to Find the Missing Word—The whole class reads the text with you or you can assign parts to be read by different children. Stop after each page. Ask, "Who thinks they can find the missing word in the pocket chart?" Make sure to have the student explain the strategy used to determine his choice. Reveal the covered word and reread the page.

**After:**
- Discussion—Talk about the animals in the story. Ask, "How many animals are there in all?" Read the text again and tally the animals to check the answers.

© Carson-Dellosa CD-2422

**Purpose:**
Create a chart of animals and their activities and sequence them.
**Preparation/Materials Needed:**
- Blank sentence strips
- Index cards
- Pocket chart
- Write the following headings on the index cards: **Animal** and **Activity**
- Place the heading cards in the pocket chart

**Before:**
- Reviewing—Ask, "What animals are in this story?" List responses in the Animal column.

**During:**
- Choral Reading—The whole class reads the text with you or you can assign parts to be read by different children.
- Finding and Writing—Find the name of each animal and the activity each one undertakes to help the pig, then write these on separate sentence strips. Place the sentence strips under the appropriate columns in the pocket chart.

**After:**
- Reviewing and Sequencing—Remove and mix up the sentence strips; then have the students place them in the correct sequence in the pocket chart.

---

**Purpose:**
Rounding Up the Rhymes.
**Preparation/Materials Needed:**
- Chart paper
- Highlighting tape
- Highlight the following words: **pig, jig, sheep, peep, cat, hat**.

**Before:**
- Discussion—Talk about rhyming words. Ask, "Did you hear any rhyming words in the book? Let's read the story again and write those words."

**During:**
- Choral Reading—The whole class reads the text with you or you can assign parts to be read by different children.
- Finding and Writing—Find the highlighted rhyming words in pairs; then write them on the chart paper. If needed, direct children to observe that there are pairs of words that rhyme using the same spelling pattern.

**After:**
- Transfer Words—Have the children underline the spelling pattern in the rhyming words. Write two words under each underlined pattern and see if students can read them. Ask, "What if I was reading and came to this word (**dig, twig; keep, sleep; mat, scat**)?"

---

**Purpose:**
Participate in Doing the Book.
**Preparation/Materials Needed:**
- The "Props"—pictures of the following characters: **pig, cow, baboon, goat, horse, sheep, yaks, parakeet, cat, walrus, duck**. Using the big book, write corresponding text for each character on the back of its picture (for example: pig, Teach me how to jig!; cow, I will you show you how; etc.).

**Before:**
- Presenting the Props—Discuss how to use the props in Doing the Book.
- Picture Walk—Confirm the actions and their sequence for Doing the Book.

**During:**
- Doing the Book—Pass out the props. The class choral reads the text. The characters read their parts at the appropriate times. Repeat, allowing every child an opportunity to participate as a character.

**After:**
- Discussion—Talk about each character in the story and tell what they did in the story.

---

## Two-Day Format:

**Before:**
- Cover Talk and Picture Walk (See Day 1, page 128.)

**During:**
- Read Aloud (See Day 1, page 128.)
- Shared Reading (See Day 1, page 128.)

**After:**
- Finding and Writing (See Day 3, page 129.)

**Before:**
- Picture Walk (See Day 1, page 128.)

**During:**
- Choral Reading to Find the Missing Word (See Day 2, page 128.)

**After:**
- Doing the Book (See Day 5, page 129 and above.)

**Predictable Chart Idea:**

A pig could learn to _____.
A pig could learn to <u>read a book</u>. (Mrs. Lafayette)
A pig could learn to <u>build a house</u>. (Jeff)
A pig could learn to <u>cook</u>. (Sue)

**Read-Aloud Books:**
- *The Musicians of Bremen* by Brenda Parkes and Judith Smith (Rigby, 1984) Only available in six-packs.
- *Sheep in a Jeep* by Nancy Shaw (Houghton Mifflin Co., 1988)
- *Farm Concert* by Joy Cowley (Wright Group, 1998)

# The Popcorn Popper

## by JoAnne Nelson
### (Modern Curriculum Press, 1992)

Harry Hopper has a new popcorn popper that will never stop. All the popcorn popping has the whole town hopping, so Harry Hopper opens up a popcorn shop.

**Purpose:**
> Build background and read for enjoyment.

**Before:**
- Picture Walk (pages 3-5 only)—Ask, "What do you notice? What could happen in this story?"

**During:**
- Reading and Thinking Aloud—Page 3: Think aloud, "I wonder why the boy is so unhappy?" Read the page and say, "That popper won't work. What is Harry going to do now?" Pages 4-5: Say, "It looks like Harry is going to get a new popcorn popper. Who's that man with Harry?" Read the pages. Say, "Wow! That man is Harry's Uncle Don. He took Harry to get a new popper. It looks like Harry is making some popcorn." Page 6: Read the page and say, "What a fantastic popcorn popper. It even sings songs." Pages 7-11: Read the pages. Ask, "What could happen next?" Finish the story.
- Shared Reading—Invite the students to join in and share the reading.

**After:**
- Discussion—Ask, "What part of *The Popcorn Popper* did you like best?"

---

**Purpose:**
> Identify the beginning, the middle, and the end of the story.

**Preparation/Materials Needed:**
- Beach Ball with questions
- Three sentence strips
- Three index cards
- Pocket chart
- Write the following headings on the index cards: **Beginning**, **Middle**, **End**.
- Place the heading cards in the pocket chart

**Before:**
- Retelling—Let children retell the story with a picture walk.

**During:**
- Echo Reading—Read a line and let the children be your echo, repeating the line after you.

**After:**
- Discussion and Writing—Ask, "What happened at the beginning of the story? In the middle? At the end?" Write the students' responses on sentence strips and place them under the correct heading in the pocket chart.
- Beach Ball Questions—Toss the beach ball. Assist the student who catches the ball in reading one of the questions. Allow students to answer the question. Encourage them to refer to the pocket chart or book cover when giving their answers.

**Purpose:**
Highlight and record all the words with the **-op** spelling pattern and make words the "Building-Blocks Way."

**Preparation/Materials Needed:**
- Highlighting tape
- Letter vests or letters cards for the following rhyming pattern and beginning sounds: **-op; t, h, r, l, b, c**

**Before:**
- Retelling—Use the cover as a catalyst for retelling the story.

**During:**
- Choral Reading and Highlighting—Assign groups and choral read in two parts. The students read "The Popcorn Popper's Song." You read the remaining text. Stop after each two-page spread. Find and highlight any words with the **-op** spelling pattern.

**After:**
- Making Words the "Building-Blocks Way"—Pass out letter vests or cards for the spelling pattern **-op**, as in **pop**. Have the three children with **o** and **p** stand together at the front of the room as you blend the sounds. Then, pass out cards for **t, h, r, l, b**, and **c**. Guide the children with these cards to the front and have them stand with the **-ook** children to make new words using the spelling pattern and the other letter cards. Be sure that **c + r** and **b + r** get together at the front, then blend their sounds together and make more words.

---

**Purpose:**
Round up the Rhymes

**Preparation/Materials Needed:**
- The following Dr. Seuss books: *Hop on Pop*; *Socks on Fox*; *The Cat in the Hat*.
- Highlighting tape
- Chart paper

**Before:**
- Introduce Rhyming Words—Use the Dr. Seuss book covers to lead a discussion about rhyming words. Make sure the students understand that rhyming words usually have the same spelling pattern, but that there are many exceptions, like **socks** and **fox**.

**During:**
- Choral Reading—Assign groups and choral read the big book in three parts. One group reads "The Popcorn Popper's Song." Another group reads all the conversation (the words in quotations marks). The final group reads the narration (the words not in quotation marks).
- Finding and Highlighting—Find all the rhyming words in the big book and highlight them. (Note: most pages have at least two pairs of rhyming words.)

**After:**
- Round up the Rhymes—Write the rhyming words on the chart paper. Use the following spelling patterns: **-op, -ong, -ock**. Each rhyme should have its own column.
- Transfer Words—Have the children underline the spelling patterns in the rhyming words. Write two words under each underlined pattern and see if students can read them. Ask, "What would you do if your were reading and came to these words (**stop, crop; long, strong; stock, shock**)?"

### Purpose:
Participate in Doing the Book.
### Preparation/Materials Needed:
- Small foam pieces used for packing boxes. These will become the popcorn during the performance.
- Popcorn bags or boxes, or small white bags
- Big box to be the popcorn popper
- Popcorn (already popped)

### Before:
- Reviewing—Talk about the story. Ask, "Who are the characters? What do they do? What happened in the beginning? In the middle? At the end?" Assign students to be the following characters: Harry, Uncle Don, Mr. Hobbs, Mayor Dodd, the popcorn popper, and narrator (remaining students).
- Script—The script for this production will be the book itself. The students who do not have an assigned part will be the narrator.

### During:
- Doing the Book—Two to three students should be inside or behind the big box throwing out packing foam when the popcorn popper is popping. Practice several times.

### After:
- Discussion—Ask, "What was your favorite part? Why?" Serve popcorn when the production has ended.

## Two-Day Format:

### Before:
- Picture Walk (See Day 1, page 131.)
### During:
- Reading and Thinking Aloud (See Day 1, page 131.)
- Shared Reading (See Day 1, page 131.)
### After:
- Discussion and Writing (See Day 2, page 131.)

### Before:
- Retelling (See Day 2, page 131.)
### During:
- Choral Reading (See Day 4, page 132.)
### After:
- Doing the Book (See Day 5, above.)

## EXTENSIONS

### Read-Aloud Books:
- *Popcorn* by Alex Moran (Harcourt, 2000)
- *The Popcorn Book* by Tomi de Paola (Holiday House, Inc., 1988)

# Pumpkin, Pumpkin

## by Jeanne Tigherington
### (Scholastic Big Books, 1986)

Jamie plants a pumpkin seed and watches it grow into a full-size pumpkin. The simple text of this book introduces children to the life cycle of a plant.

**Purpose:**
Build background knowledge and read for enjoyment.

**Before:**
- Cover Talk—Ask, "What do you notice? What is the dog doing? What could happen in this story?"
- Picture Walk—Start a discussion of each page with the question, "What do you notice?" Talk about the pictures. Remind the students to use the pictures to help decode new or unknown words.

**During:**
- Read Aloud—Read the big book aloud to the students with full expression.
- Shared Reading—Invite the students to join in and share the reading.

**After:**
- Discussion—Ask, "What did you learn about pumpkins?"

---

**Purpose:**
Reread the story and discuss what this book is about: pumpkins.

**Preparation/Materials Needed:**
- Highlighting tape

**Before:**
- Retelling—Allow students to retell the story during a picture walk.
- Predictions—Predict how many times the word **pumpkin** will appear in the text.

**During:**
- Choral Reading and Highlighting—The whole class reads the text with you or you can assign parts to be read by different children. Stop after each two-page spread. Allow students to find, highlight, and tally the word **pumpkin**.

**After:**
- Discussion—Talk about how many times you found the word **pumpkin** in the big book. Then, talk about the life cycle of a pumpkin.

### Purpose:
Use context, picture clues, and beginning letter sounds to Guess the Covered Word.

### Preparation/Materials Needed:
- Self-stick notes
- Place self-stick notes on the following words in the story: **seed**, **sprout**, **flower**, **plant**, **pulp**, **face**.

### Before:
- Retelling—Use the cover as a catalyst for retelling the story.

### During:
- Choral Reading to Guess the Covered Word—Choral read each page. Take suggestions for the covered word, then uncover the beginning sound. Take additional suggestions if needed. Reveal the covered word, then reread the page.

### After:
- Discussion—Talk about planting pumpkin seeds. Let students share any experiences they have had with pumpkins.
- Drawing—Draw a picture of a seed and label the parts.

### Purpose:
Create a life-cycle chart for Jamie's pumpkin seed.

### Preparation/Materials Needed:
- Pocket chart
- Sentence strips

### Before:
- Discussion and Writing—Ask, "What happens when you plant a pumpkin seed?" Write the suggestions on sentence strips. Discuss if the sentence strip should be placed in the beginning, middle, or end of the pocket chart. Finally, place the sentence strip in the pocket chart.

### During:
- Choral Reading—The whole class reads the text with you or you can assign parts to be read by different children. Stop at the end of each two-page spread. Ask, "What happened on these pages? Is this something we need to add to our chart?" Write any new steps on sentence strips and add them to the pocket chart.

### After:
- Discussion—Talk about the life cycle of a pumpkin. Model how to retell the story using the life-cycle chart, and invite children to retell the story also.

### Purpose:
Visit a pumpkin farm or fruit stand to get pumpkins for carving and roasting seeds. If the class can't do this, bring a pumpkin to school.

### Preparation/Materials Needed:
- Utensils for carving the pumpkins in school (Think safety!)
- One adult helper per pumpkin (if possible and necessary for multiple pumpkins)
- Margarine and salt for roasting seeds
- Baking sheet
- Toaster oven or oven in the school cafeteria

**Before:**
- Discussion—Talk about carving a pumpkin: what you will do and how you will do it.
- Predictions—Predict how many seeds are in the pumpkin.

**During:**
- Directions—Write directions for carving a pumpkin. For example: 1. Draw a pattern on the pumpkin. 2. Cut a hole in the top of the pumpkin. etc.

**After:**
- Carving the Pumpkin—Scoop out the insides of the pumpkins and save the seeds. If you have more than one pumpkin, have an adult help carve the pumpkins. Count the pumpkin seeds and check the answer. Roast the pumpkin seeds. Have some of the seeds for a snack and send the remaining seeds home as souvenirs with the students.

## Two-Day Format:

**Before:**
- Cover Talk and Picture Walk (See Day 1, page 134.)

**During:**
- Read Aloud (See Day 1, page 134.)
- Shared Reading (See Day 1, page 134.)

**After:**
- Discussion (See Day 1, page 134.)

**Before:**
- Picture Walk (See Day 1, page 134.)

**During:**
- Choral Reading to Guess the Covered Word (See Day 3, page 135.)

**After:**
- Discussion and Writing (See Day 4, page 135.)

**Math:**
Predict how many seeds are in a pumpkin. Count and tally. Group the seeds into tens and ones. Count again.

**Read-Aloud Books:**
- *It's Pumpkin Time* by Zoe Hall and Shari Halpern (Scholastic, Inc., 1999)
- *Too Many Pumpkins* by Linda White (Holiday House, Inc., 1997)
- *Apples and Pumpkins* by Anne Rockwell (Simon and Schuster Children's, 1994)
- *Pumpkin Day, Pumpkin Night* by Anne Rockwell (Walker and Co., 1999)

# Quick as a Cricket

## by Audrey Wood
### (Child's Play, 1982)

A young child explores the versatility of being a human being. The boy, mimicking different kinds of animals, shows individual feelings, character traits, and actions that every person can relate to. Donald Wood's illustrations add charm to his wife's whimsical rhyming text.

**Purpose:**
Build background and read for enjoyment.

**Before:**
- Cover Talk—Ask, "What do you notice? What kind of animal is on the cover?" Discuss a cricket's ability to jump and make sound.
- Picture Walk—Start a discussion of each page with the question, "What do you notice?" Talk about the pictures and the words.

**During:**
- Read Aloud—Read the big book aloud to the students with full expression.
- Shared Reading—Invite the students to join in and share the reading.

**After:**
- Discussion—Talk about the animals and the actions in the book. As students return to their seats, have them tell you how the animals in this book might return to their seats. Ask, "How would a cricket go back to its seat? (quick) How would a snail return to its seat? (slow)."

---

**Purposes:**
Use context, picture clues, and memory to Find the Missing Words.
Sequence the events in the big book.

**Preparation/Materials Needed:**
- Self-stick notes
- Index cards
- Pocket chart
- Place self-stick notes on the following words: **snail, whale, lark, shark, fox, ox, clam, lamb, shrimp, chimp, bee, me**.
- Write the missing words on index cards and place them in the pocket chart.

**Before:**
- Retelling—Allow children to retell the story during a picture walk.

**During:**
- Choral Reading to Find the Missing Word—Choral read each page. Take student suggestions for the covered word and read the sentence using each suggested word. Reveal the covered word and reread the page.

**After:**
- Sequencing—Let students place the index cards in the order the animals appear in the book. Read the text, stopping occasionally at an important word which the students should read. Check to see if the index cards are sequenced correctly.

---

**Purpose:**
List the animals and their unique characteristics.

**Preparation/Materials Needed:**
- Chart paper
- On the chart paper, create a three-column chart with the following headings: **Animal; How did the animal act?; What will we do?**

**Before:**
- Reviewing—Ask, "What animals were in the story?" List the students' responses on the chart.

**During:**
- Choral Reading—The whole class reads the text with you or you can assign parts to be read by different children. Check to see if everyone remembers all the animals.

**After:**
- Finding and Writing—Find the animals and their actions; then write them under the appropriate columns on the chart.
- Discussion—Talk about the animals and their actions. Create pantomime actions the class can do for each animal.

---

**Purpose:**
Round Up the Rhymes and use spelling patterns to read and write new words.

**Preparation/Materials Needed:**
- Chart paper or transparency
- Chart from Day 3
- Highlighting tape
- Highlight the following words in the big book: **lark, shark, shrimp, chimp.**

**Before:**
- Reviewing—Use the chart created on Day 3 (above) to act out the book. For example, say, "The cricket is quick," while the children run in place.

**During:**
- Choral Reading—The whole class reads the text with you or you can assign parts to be read by different children. Ask, "What did you notice today as we read the story? Which words were highlighted?"

**After:**
- Finding and Writing—Find the highlighted words and write them on chart paper or a transparency. If needed, direct children to observe that there are pairs of words that rhyme using the same spelling pattern.
- Transfer Words—Have the children underline the spelling pattern in the rhyming words. Write two words under each underlined pattern and see if students can read them. Ask, "What if I was reading and came to this word (**dark, spark; limp, skimp**)?"

---

**Purpose:**
Participate in Doing the Book.

**Preparation/Materials Needed:**
- One index card for each child
- Write the following words on the index cards, one word per card: **quick, slow, small, large, sad, happy, nice, mean, cold, hot, weak, strong, loud, quiet, tough, gentle, brave, shy, tame, wild, lazy, busy, in, out, up, down.**
- Pocket chart

**Before:**
- Picture Walk—Discuss what happened in the big book and the actions of each animal.

**During:**
- Choral Reading—The whole class reads the text with you or you can assign parts to be read by different children. Add the actions from the chart created on Day 3 (page 138).

**After:**
- Matching Opposites—Talk about the opposites in this story. Give each student an index card. You should keep the "up" card which will be used to start the activity. Select a student to show her card. Discuss what word is on the card and how students knew the word. Place the card in the pocket chart. Ask, "What is the opposite of (the word)?" Then, ask, "What sound does (the word) begin with? Let's all say that sound." Next, ask, "What letter says (that sound)?" Finally, ask, "Who can find (the letter) on the alphabet chart?" (Allow the child to use a pointer to locate the letter on the alphabet chart.) Go back to the pocket chart, point, and ask, "Does anyone think they have the card that is the opposite of (the word)?" Have the student place the word in the pocket next to its opposite. Continue until all the cards have been placed in the pocket chart.
- Creating a Class Book—Pass out the index cards. Each child will copy the word on their card and create an illustration for the word. Combine the pages with the correct opposite and bind them into a class book.

## Two-Day Format:

**Before:**
- Cover Talk and Picture Walk (See Day 1, page 137.)

**During:**
- Read Aloud (See Day 1, page 137.)
- Shared Reading (See Day 1, page 137.)

**After:**
- Finding and Writing (See Day 3, page 138.)

**Before:**
- Picture Walk (See Day 1, page 137.)

**During:**
- Choral Reading (See Day 3, page 138.)

**After:**
- Discussion (See Day 3, page 138.)
- Matching Opposites (See Day 5, above.)

# EXTENSIONS

**Predictable Chart Idea:**

_____ is as _____ as a _____.
Ms. Seely is as silly as a monkey.
Allison is as sneaky as a snake.
Ivan is as wiggly as a worm.

# Shoes from Grandpa

## by Mem Fox
### (Harcourt School, 1989)

Grandpa notices that Jessie has grown a lot. He realizes she will need new shoes and he provides them. As a result, the rest of the family lends a helping hand in creating a new wardrobe for Jessie.

**Purpose:**
Build background and read for enjoyment.

**Before:**
• Cover Talk—Ask, "What do you notice? Why do you think the story is titled *Shoes from Grandpa*?"

**During:**
• Read Aloud—Read the big book aloud to the students with full expression.
• Shared Reading—Invite the students to join in and share the reading.

**After:**
• Discussion—Talk about the book, then make a web with types of clothing children need.

---

**Purpose:**
Reread the book and discuss the names of clothing in the big book.

**Preparation/Materials Needed:**
• Self-stick notes
• Index cards
• Pocket chart
• Place self-stick notes on names of clothing in the big book.
• Write the names of clothing on index cards, and place the index cards in the pocket chart.

**Before:**
• Retelling—Allow the students to retell the story during a picture walk. Talk about the clothes on each page.

**During:**
• Choral Reading to Find the Missing Word—The whole class reads the text with you or you can assign parts to be read by different children. Stop after each page. Ask, "Who thinks they can find the missing word from this page in the pocket chart?" Make sure to have the students explain the strategies used to determine their choices. Reveal the covered word and reread the page.

**After:**
• Discussion—Talk about all the clothes you found in the book.
• Writing and Drawing—Let the children write the names of pieces of clothing. Then, let them draw pictures of the clothing.

**Purpose:**
Discuss family members and highlight the names of family members.
**Preparation/Materials Needed:**
- Highlighting tape

**Before:**
- Retelling—Use the cover as a catalyst for retelling the story. Talk about the people (characters) in the book.

**During:**
- Echo Reading—Read a line and let the children be your echo, repeating the line after you.
- Choral Reading and Highlighting—The whole class reads the text with you or you can assign parts to be read by different children. Stop after each two-page spread. Allow students to find and highlight the names of family members. Be sure to talk with students about how they located the names.

**After:**
- Writing and Drawing—Let the children complete the following sentence: _____ was wearing a _____. Then, let them illustrate their sentences. Put the pages together to make a class book.

---

**Purpose:**
Round Up the Rhymes and use spelling patterns to read some new words.
**Preparation/Materials Needed:**
- Highlight the following words: **coat, boat, hat, that, mean, jeans**.
- Chart paper or transparency

**Before:**
- Discussion—Talk about the story and rhyming words. Have the children listen for rhyming words as they read the story again.

**During:**
- Choral Reading—The whole class reads the text with you or you can assign parts to be read by different children.

**After:**
- Finding and Writing—Ask, "What did you notice today as we read the story?" Find the rhyming words and highlight them. Write the highlighted words on chart paper or a transparency. If needed, direct children to observe that there are pairs of words that rhyme using the same spelling pattern.
- Transfer Words—Have the children underline the spelling pattern in the rhyming words. Write two words under each underlined pattern and see if students can read them. Ask, "What if I was reading and came to this word (**goat, float; hat, flat; bean, clean**)?"

---

**Purpose:**
Participate in Doing the Book.

**Preparation/Materials Needed:**
- The "Props"—Gather or draw pictures of the following items: **shoes, socks, skirt, blouse, sweater, coat, scarf, hat, mittens, jeans**. Label each picture on the front with the character associated with that item, then write two lines of dialogue for each character on the back of the picture. For example: on the front of the **shoes** picture write **Grandpa**; on the back of the **shoes** picture, write, "**1st: Jessie you've grown, I'll get you some shoes.**" and "**Other: to go with the shoes from Grandpa.**" On the front of the **socks** picture write **Dad**; on the back of the **socks** picture write, "**1st: I'll get you socks from the local shops.**" and "**Other: to go with the socks from the local shops.**"; etc.

**Before:**
- Discussion—Talk about the characters in the story. Ask, "How many characters are there? Who are the characters?" Talk about what each character will say and do when the class is Doing the Book.

**During:**
- Choral Reading—Assign groups and choral read in two parts. One group reads the repetitive text. The other group reads the remaining text.
- Doing the Book—Pass out the pictures and have students sit in the proper sequence. Start by saying, "Grandpa said," and touches the first student's head. The first student jumps up and reads the first line. Move to the next student, and say, "Then, dad said." Dad then reads his first line, followed by Grandpa saying his other line. Move to the next student and say, "Mom said." Mom then reads her first line, followed by Dad and Grandpa reading their other lines. Continue in this fashion until the end of the story. Repeat this activity until everyone in the class has participated.

**After:**
- Writing and Drawing—Let students complete the following sentence: In this book, Jessie got new _____. Finish by illustrating the sentence.

## Two-Day Format:

**Before:**
- Cover Talk (See Day 1, page 140.)

**During:**
- Read Aloud (See Day 1, page 140.)
- Shared Reading (See Day 1, page 140.)

**After:**
- Writing and Drawing (See Day 3, page 141.)

**Before:**
- Picture Walk (See Day 1, page 140.)

**During:**
- Echo Reading (See Day 3, page 141.)
- Choral Reading (See Day 4, page 141.)

**After:**
- Doing the Book (See Day 5, page 141 and above.)

**Predictable Chart Idea:**
My _____ gave me _____.
My wife gave me a new shirt. (Mr. Young)
My brother gave me a lollipop. (Patrick)
My dad gave me a new bike. (Lynn)

142 © Carson-Dellosa CD-2422

# Silly Sally

## by Audrey Wood
### (Harcourt Brace, 1992)

When Silly Sally goes to town, she goes in a most unusual manner . . . walking backwards, upside down. Along the way, Sally meets several other characters that join in the unique backwards, upside-down parade. Soon the topsy-turvy group meets a sheep and they all fall asleep. Never fear . . . the delightfully illustrated Neddy Buttercup awakens the slumbering bunch. The group proceeds to town and, of course, they are all walking backwards, upside down!

**Purpose:**
Build background knowledge and read for enjoyment.

**Before:**
- Cover Talk—Ask, "What do you notice? What is the woman doing? What do you think her name is? Why do you think the story is titled *Silly Sally*? What could happen in this story?"
- Picture Walk—Start a discussion of each page with the question, "What do you notice?" Talk about the pictures and any new words the pictures help you with.

**During:**
- Read Aloud—Read the big book aloud to the students with full expression.
- Shared Reading—Invite the students to join in and share the reading.

**After:**
- Discussion—Ask, "What other silly ways could Sally have gone to town?"

---

**Purpose:**
Read the book to Find the Missing Words and talk about those words.

**Preparation/Materials Needed:**
- Self-stick notes
- Place self-stick notes on the following words: **walking, danced, dancing, played, leaping, sang, singing, fell, sleeping, tickled, woke.**

**Before:**
- Retelling—Allow children to retell the story during a picture walk.

**During:**
- Choral Reading to Find the Missing Word—The whole class reads the text with you or you can assign parts to be read by different children. Stop at the end of each page. Take student suggestions for the covered word, and read the sentence using each suggested word. Reveal the covered word, and reread the page.

**After:**
- Discussion—Talk about all the action words in this story. Let the children mimic each action.

## Purpose:
Find the animals in the big book and discuss what they did.
## Preparation/Materials Needed:
- Highlighting tape

**Before:**
- Retelling—Use the cover as a catalyst for retelling the story. Ask, "What are some of characters in the story?" Inform students that they will be searching for animal names while they read.

**During:**
- Echo Reading—Read a line and let the children be your echo, repeating the line after you.
- Choral Reading and Highlighting—The whole class reads the text with you or you can assign parts to be read by different children. Stop after each two-page spread. Allow students to find and highlight the animal names.

**After:**
- Discussion—Talk about all the animals in the big book and what they did in the story.

## Purpose:
Identify the beginning, the middle, and the end of the story.
## Preparation/Materials Needed:
- Beach Ball with questions
- Three sentence strips
- Three index cards
- Pocket chart
- Write the following headings on the index cards: **Beginning**, **Middle**, **End**.
- Place the heading cards in the pocket chart.

**Before:**
- Reviewing—Talk about the story you read on Day 1 (page 143). When you read today, think aloud about the beginning, the middle, and the end.

**During:**
- Choral Read—Assign groups and choral read in two parts, alternating pages.

**After:**
- Discussion and Writing—Ask, "What happened at the beginning? In the middle? At the end?" Write the responses on sentence strips and place them under the correct headings in the pocket chart.
- Beach Ball Questions—Toss the beach ball. Assist the student who catches the ball in reading one of the questions. Allow students to answer the question. Encourage them to refer to the pocket chart or book cover when giving their answers.

## Purpose:
Create a chart of characters and their actions.
## Preparation/Materials Needed:
- Pictures of animals presented in the text
- Chart paper
- On the chart paper, start a chart with the headings: **Character** and **Action**

**Before:**
- Reviewing—Ask, "What characters did we meet in this story?" List student responses in the Character column of the chart.

**During:**
- Choral Reading—Assign groups and choral read in two parts, alternating the reading of pages.

**After:**
- Discussion—Talk about the characters and actions.
- Finding and Writing—Find the character names and their actions, then write them on the chart.
- Extending the Chart—Create pantomime actions for each character. Perform the pantomime actions while choral reading the book.

---

## Two-Day Format:

**Before:**
- Cover Talk and Picture Walk (See Day 1, page 143.)

**During:**
- Read Aloud (See Day 1, page 143.)
- Shared Reading (See Day 1, page 143.)

**After:**
- Discussion and Writing (See Day 4, page 144.)

**Before:**
- Picture Walk (See Day 1, page 143.)

**During:**
- Choral Reading to Find the Missing Word (See Day 2, page 143.)

**After:**
- Discussion (See Day 5, above.)
- Finding and Writing (See Day 5, above.)

### Read-Aloud Books:
- *The Musicians of Bremen* by Brenda Parkes and Judith Smith (Rigby, 1984) Only available in six-packs.
- *Make Way for Ducklings* by Robert McCloskey (Viking Children's Books, 1976)
- *Rosie's Walk* by Pat Hutchins (Simon & Schuster Children's, 1968)
- *We're Going on a Bear Hunt* by Michael Rosen (Simon & Schuster Children's, 1989)

# Splish, Splash

## by Jeff Sheppard
### (Harcourt School, 1994)

Squeak, splash! Moo, splash! Meow, splash! Ribbit, splash! One animal after another topples into the lake. Some like it and some don't. However, children will love this playful rhyme about animals and their sounds.

**Purpose:**
Build background knowledge and read for enjoyment.

**Before:**
- Cover Talk—Ask, "What do you notice? What are the frog and the cat doing? What could happen in this story?"
- Picture Walk—Start a discussion of each page with the question, "What do you notice?" Talk about the pictures and some important words.

**During:**
- Read Aloud—Read the big book aloud to the students with full expression.
- Shared Reading—Invite the students to join in and share the reading.

**After:**
- Name that Animal—Play the "Name that Animal" game. For example, say, "Name the animal that said, 'Quack, splash!'" (duck) or "Name the animal the got water in its eyes." (mouse).

---

**Purpose:**
Read the big book again, talk about the story, and highlight and tally each occurrence of the word **splash**.

**Preparation/Materials Needed:**
- Highlighting tape
- Letter vests or letter cards for the following rhyming pattern and beginning sounds: **-ash**; **b, c, r, d, l, m, s, t**

**Before:**
- Retelling—Allow students to retell the story during a picture walk.
- Predictions—Predict how many times the word **splash** will appear in the text.

**During:**
- Choral Reading—The whole class reads the text with you or you can assign parts to be read by different children. Stop after each two-page spread. Allow students to find, highlight, and tally the word **splash**.

**After:**
- Making Words the "Building-Blocks Way"—Pass out letter vests or cards for the spelling pattern **-ash**, as in **splash**. Have the three children with **a, s,** and **h** stand together at the front of the room as you blend the sounds. Then, pass out cards for **b, c, r, d, l, m, s,** and **t**. Guide the children with these cards to the front and have them stand with the **-ash** children to make new words using the spelling pattern and the other letter cards. Be sure that **c + r, s + m,** and **t + r** get together at the front, then blend their sounds together and make more words.

**Purpose:**
Match the animal names with the appropriate sound.

**Preparation/Materials Needed:**
- Index cards
- Write each animal name and each animal sound from the big book on an index card.
- Randomly place all the completed index cards (names and sounds) in a pocket chart.

**Before:**
- Matching the Animals and Sounds—Picture walk through the book, stopping at each two-page spread. Ask, "What animal is on these pages?" Have a student locate the index card with the animal name on it. Ask, "What sound does the animal on these pages make?" Have another student locate the index card with the sound on it. Pair the animal name and sound together in the pocket chart.

**During:**
- Choral Reading—Assign groups and choral read in two parts. One group reads the animal sounds. The other group reads the remaining text, listening for all the animals and sounds.

**After:**
- Discussion—Talk about the animals and sounds. Mix up the index cards and have students match them. Use the book to check the pairings.

---

**Purpose:**
Round Up the Rhymes and use spelling patterns to read some new words.

**Preparation/Materials Needed:**
- Chart paper
- Index cards from Day 3
- Highlighting tape
- Highlight the following words in the big book: **cake, lake, grim, swim, all, small, feet, sweet**.

**Before:**
- Reviewing—Mix up the index cards from Day 3 (above) and have students match each animal name with its sound.

**During:**
- Choral Reading—The whole class reads the text with you or you can assign parts to be read by different children. Have the students listen for rhyming words as they read. Ask, "What did you notice today as we read the story? Which words were highlighted?"

**After:**
- Finding and Writing—Find the highlighted rhyming words, then write them on the chart paper. If needed, direct children to observe that there are pairs of words that rhyme using the same spelling pattern.
- Transfer Words—Have the children underline the spelling pattern in the rhyming words. Write two words under each underlined pattern and see if students can read them. Ask, "What if I was reading and came to this word (**bake, flake; Jim, trim; wall, stall; meet, fleet**)?"

**Purpose:**
Participate in Doing the Book.
**Preparation/Materials Needed:**
- The "Props"—pictures of a **bee, mouse, pig, dog, duck, cat, frog**

**Before:**
- Presenting the Props—Discuss how to use the props in Doing the Book.
- Picture Walk—Confirm the actions and their sequence for Doing the Book.

**During:**
- Doing the Book—Pass out the character cards. The class choral reads the text while the characters pantomime the actions and make the animal sounds at the appropriate time. Repeat, allowing every child to participate in the pantomime.

**After:**
- Discussion—Talk about which parts the students liked best in the story.

---

# Two-Day Format:

**Before:**
- Cover Talk and Picture Walk (See Day 1, page 146.)

**During:**
- Read Aloud (See Day 1, page 146.)
- Shared Reading (See Day 1, page 146.)

**After:**
- Name that Animal (See Day 1, page 146.)

**Before:**
- Matching the Animals and Sounds (See Day 3, page 147.)

**During:**
- Choral Reading (See Day 4, page 147.)

**After:**
- Doing the Book (See Day 5, above.)

**Predictable Chart Idea:**
_____ fell into the water and said, "_____."
Mrs. Miller fell into the water and said, "That water is really cold."
Tijuan fell into the water and said, "Oh No! I'm all wet!"
Kaitlyn fell into the water and said, "This is fun!"

---

*Shared Reading with Big Books*

© Carson-Dellosa CD-2422

# Three Little Kittens

## by Paul Galdone
### (Houghton Mifflin, 1986)

A wonderfully illustrated retelling of the classic tale of three mischievous kittens who struggle to please their mother.

**Purpose:**
Build background and read for enjoyment.

**Before:**
- Cover Talk—Ask, "What do you notice? What are the kittens wearing? Why do you think they are smiling?"
- Picture Walk—Start a discussion of each page with the question, "What do you notice?" Talk about the pictures and the words.

**During:**
- Read Aloud—Read the big book aloud to the students with full expression.
- Shared Reading—Invite the students to join in and share the reading.

**After:**
- Discussion—Ask, "What would you do if you lost your mittens?"

---

**Purpose:**
Use context, picture clues, and beginning letters to Guess the Covered Word; then read and sequence the story.

**Preparation/Materials Needed:**
- Self-stick notes
- Sentence strips
- Pocket chart
- Place self-stick notes on the following words: **lost, found, soiled, washed.**
- Write the following sentences on sentence strips: **The mittens are lost. The mittens are found. The mittens are soiled. The mittens are washed.**

**Before:**
- Retelling—Allow children to retell the story during a picture walk.

**During:**
- Choral Reading to Guess the Covered Word—The whole class reads the text with you or you can assign parts to be read by different children. Stop at the end of each page. Take suggestions for the covered word, then uncover the beginning sound. Take additional suggestions if needed. Reveal the covered word, then reread the page.

**After:**
- Sequencing—Read the sentence strips and place them in the correct sequence in the pocket chart.

---

**Purpose:**
List the kittens' good and bad behaviors.
**Preparation/Materials Needed:**
- Chart paper
- Start a chart with the following headings: **Naughty Kittens** and **Good Kittens**.

**Before:**
- Retelling—Use the cover of the big book as a catalyst for retelling the story.

**During:**
- Echo Reading—Read a line and let the children be your echo, repeating the line after you.

**After:**
- Discussion and Writing—Ask, "What naughty things did the kittens do?" Write students' responses on the chart. Then, ask, "What good things did the kittens do?" Write students' responses on the chart.

**Purpose:**
Participate in Doing the Book.
**Preparation/Materials Needed:**
- White construction paper
- Cut construction paper mittens; a pair of each student.
- Pair the mittens and attach two mittens to opposite ends of a piece of yarn.

**Before:**
- Coloring—Have students color one side of the mittens to look clean and the other side to look dirty.
- Picture Walk—Confirm the actions and their sequence for Doing the Book.

**During:**
- Doing the Book—Assign groups and choral read in two parts. Half of the students are kittens, and the other half are the mother cat. Switch parts and read the book again.

**After:**
- Discussion—Talk about your favorite part of the story.
- Writing and Drawing—Have students complete the following sentence: My favorite part of *Three Little Kittens* was _____. Then, let the students illustrate their completed sentences.

**Purpose:**
Participate in Doing the Book for an audience (invite a neighboring class).
**Preparation/Materials Needed:**
- Mittens from Day 4 (above)

**Before:**
- Reviewing the Story—Review the story and the actions, then practice Doing the Book.

**Before:**
- Doing the Book—Assign groups and choral read in two parts. Half of the students are kittens, and the other half are the mother cat.

**After:**
- Feedback—Let the visiting students tell what they liked about the story.

## Two-Day Format:

**Before:**
- Cover Talk and Picture Walk (See Day 1, page 149.)

**During:**
- Read Aloud (See Day 1, page 149.)
- Shared Reading (See Day 1, page 149.)

**After:**
- Discussion and Writing (See Day 3, page 150.)

**Before:**
- Picture Walk (See Day 1, page 149.)

**During:**
- Echo Reading (See Day 3, page 150.)
- Choral Reading to Guess the Covered Word (See Day 2, page 149.)

**After:**
- Doing the Book (See Day 4, page 150.)

 **XTENSIONS**

**Predictable Chart Idea:**
The (animal name) lost its _____.
The <u>elephant</u> lost its <u>trunk</u>. (Mrs. Lake)
The <u>tiger</u> lost its <u>stripes</u>. (David)
The <u>bird</u> lost its <u>wings</u>. (Deb)

# Today Is Monday

## by Eric Carle
### (Philomel, 1993)

Eric Carle's simple text and dazzling illustrations bring to life the children's song "Today Is Monday." The dinner menu for each day of the week is announced by one of many delightful animals. Each animal also repeats the menus for all the previous days.

**Purpose:**
Build background knowledge and read for enjoyment.

**Preparation/Materials Needed:**
- Pocket chart with the days of the week and the foods from the big book written on sentence strips
- Music for the song "Today is Monday" would be helpful.

**Before:**
- Cover Talk—Ask, "What do you notice? What is the cat doing? What do you think the cat would like to eat? Have we read any other books by the author of this book?"
- Picture Walk—Start a discussion of each page with the question, "What do you notice?" Talk about the pictures and any words you need to help children decode.

**During:**
- Read Aloud—Read the big book aloud to the students with full expression.
- Shared Reading—Invite the students to join in and share the reading.

**After:**
- Discussion—Talk about what happened each day in the book. Use the prepared pocket chart to introduce the song "Today is Monday."

---

**Purpose:**
Use context, picture clues, and onset to Find the Missing Words.

**Preparation/Materials Needed:**
- Self-stick notes
- Index cards
- Pocket chart
- Place self-stick notes on the following words: **string beans**, **spaghetti**, **zooop**, **roast beef**, **fresh fish**, **chicken**, **ice cream**.
- Write the covered words on index cards.
- Place the index cards in the pocket chart.

**Before:**
- Retelling—Allow students to retell the story during a picture walk.

**During:**
- Choral Reading to Find the Missing Words—The whole class reads the text with you or you can assign parts to be read by different children. Stop after each page. Ask, "Who thinks they can find the missing word in the pocket chart?" Make sure to have the student explain the strategy used to determine her choice. Reveal the covered word and reread the page.

**After:**
- Discussion—Talk about the words the students found. Have them write and draw the words.

**Purpose:**
List the days of the week, the food eaten, and the animals on a chart.

**Preparation/Materials Needed:**
- Pocket chart
- Index cards
- Use index cards to create the following headings: **Day**, **Food**, and **Animal**.
- Write the following words from the big book on additional index cards: the days of the week, the foods eaten on those days, and the animals which introduced the days/food.

**Before:**
- Sequencing—Place the days of the week randomly in the correct column in the pocket chart. Have students suggest how to sequence them correctly.

**During:**
- Choral Read—The whole class reads the text with you or you can assign parts to be read by different children. Check the sequence for the days of the week.

**After:**
- Completing the Chart—Find the food that was eaten on each day in the text. Then, find the index card that has the same word on it. Place the food index cards in the correct column in the pocket chart. Find the name of the animal for each day of the week in the text. Then, find the index card that has the same word on it. Place the animal index cards in the correct column in the pocket chart.
- Extending the Chart—Mix up the cards from two columns and pass them out to the class. Have the students place them correctly in the pocket chart. Use the book to check the completed chart.

**Purpose:**
Participate in Doing the Book.

**Preparation/Materials Needed:**
- The "Props"—pictures of each food in the story. Be sure to have two to four cards for each food (enough for each student to have a card).

**Before:**
- Presenting the Props—Discuss how to use the props in Doing the Book.
- Picture Walk—Confirm the actions and their sequence for Doing the Book.

**During:**
- Doing the Book—Pass out the props to the students. As the class choral reads the text, the students will hold up their food cards at the appropriate time. Repeat and present to an audience.

**After:**
- Singing—Sing the song, "Today is Monday."
- Writing and Drawing—Talk about the students' favorite days in the big book. Have students complete the following sentence: My favorite day was _____. Then, let the students illustrate their completed sentences.

**Purpose:**
Create an interactive chart for the song, "Today is Monday."

**Preparation/Materials Needed:**
- Pocket chart from Day 3 (above)
- Chart paper

**Before:**
- Reviewing—Mix up the cards from two columns and pass them out. Have the students place them correctly in the chart. Use the book to check the completed chart.

**During:**
- Choral Reading—Assign groups and choral read in two parts. One group reads the name of the food. The other group reads the remaining text.

**After:**
- Interactive Chart—List the days of the week on chart paper. Start with Monday at the bottom. Randomly select a student and ask, "What would you like to eat on Monday?" Record her response on the chart. Continue for the other days of the week.

## Two-Day Format:

**Before:**
- Cover Talk and Picture Walk (See Day 1, page 152.)

**During:**
- Read Aloud (See Day 1, page 152.)
- Shared Reading (See Day 1, page 152.)

**After:**
- Discussion (See Day 2, page 152.)

**Before:**
- Picture Walk (See Day 1, page 152.)

**During:**
- Choral Reading to Find the Missing Words (See Day 2, page 152.)

**After:**
- Interactive Chart (See Day 5, above.)

**Predictable Chart Idea:**

I would like to eat _____ every day.

I would like to eat <u>linguine</u> every day. (Ms. Lawbook)

I would like to eat <u>hot dogs</u> every day. (Dannie)

I would like to eat <u>pizza</u> every day. (Mary B.)

# Where Does Breakfast Come From?

## by David Flint
### (Rigby, 1998)

Children will learn the process that occurs in bringing milk, eggs, bread, cornflakes, and orange juice to the breakfast table. This book includes many elements common in nonfiction text, including a table of contents, an index, page titles, sequenced pictures with captions, and a chart.

**Purpose:**
  Build background knowledge and read for enjoyment.
**Preparation/Materials Needed:**
  • Chart paper

**Before:**
  • Cover Talk—Ask, "What do you notice? What kinds of foods are in the picture? What meal do you think is on the table? Is the word breakfast on the cover? Where? How did you know that word was breakfast?"
  • Building Background Knowledge and Making Connections—Create a web of breakfast words and ideas. Place breakfast in the center of the chart paper (you can be creative—make the center of your web look like a plate or a fried egg!). Ask, "What are some words you think about when I say, 'breakfast'?" Write the student responses on the web. Ask "What do you think we will learn by reading this book?"

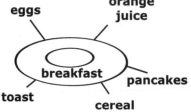

**During:**
  • Read Aloud—Read the big book aloud to the students with full expression.
  • Shared Reading—Invite the students to join in and share the reading.
**After:**
  • Discussion—Talk about what you had for breakfast (be sure it was a healthy breakfast!). Ask one student, "What is one thing you had for breakfast today?" (For example: I had toast.) Ask, "Who else had (toast)?" Dismiss the students who had toast to their seats. Repeat the activity until all the students have returned to their seats.

**Purpose:**
  Introduce or review the elements of nonfiction text.

**Before:**
  • Retelling—Allow children to retell the story during a picture walk.
**During:**
  • Echo Reading—Read a line and let the children be your echo, repeating the line after you.
  • Introducing Nonfiction Elements—Show and discuss the following elements as the class choral reads the story: **Table of Contents**; **Headings**; **Number Sequencing**; **Chart**; **Index**.
**After:**
  • Discussion—Talk about how the table of contents and the index help readers. Have children locate information using the index and/or the table of contents. For example, "How can the table of contents be used to find information about milk?"

### Purpose:
Use the table of contents to find information to add to the web. Summarize a section of the book.

### Preparation/Materials Needed:
• Web from Day 1

**Before:**
• Reviewing—Say, "Let's look at the web we made for breakfast words on Monday (Day 1, page 155). What items are both on our web and in the book?"

**During:**
• Setting a Purpose—Say, "Today let's read to find more information to add to the web for each type of breakfast food in the book. There is a page in this book that tells us all the different topics this book contains. Does anybody remember what that page is called?" (table of contents).
• Locating Information—Have the students choral read the book with you. Stop after each page to locate the information about each food item.

**After:**
• Adding to the Web—After reading the section, the students should suggest additions to the web.
• Summarizing—Write a summary with the class of one section of the book. Model how to use the web to orally summarize a section of the book. Allow some students to try making their own summaries for the other sections.

---

### Purpose:
Sequence a summary of the book.

### Preparation/Materials Needed:
• Pocket chart
• Five sentence strips
• Write "Where does breakfast come from?" on one side of each of the five sentence strips. On the opposite side of each sentence strip, write one of the following sentences: The milk comes from cows. The bread comes from flour. The flour comes from wheat. The cornflakes come from corn. The orange juice comes from oranges.

**Before:**
• Reviewing—Talk about what happened in each section of the big book.

**During:**
• Choral Reading— Assign groups and choral read in two parts. One group reads the headings. The other group reads the remaining text.

**After:**
• Sequencing—Sequence the sentence strips in the pocket chart.
• Being the Book—Pass out the sentence strips and arrange the students in the correct sequence. Have the students read their sentence strips or read the sentence strips chorally.

---

### Purpose:
Make and eat breakfast.

### Preparation/Materials Needed:
• Orange juice, milk, and cornflakes
• Disposable cups, bowls, spoons, and napkins
• Chart paper
• Write the breakfast menu on the chart paper.

---

**Before:**
- Building Background Knowledge—Share an experience of having to read the school's lunch or breakfast menu.

**During:**
- Shared Reading—Read the menu together. Ask, "What do you notice about today's menu?" Make sure the entire menu is discussed and read.

**After:**
- Let's Eat—Enjoy this breakfast together.
- Writing and Drawing—Each student completes the following sentence: For breakfast, I like _____. Then, have each student illustrate his sentence. Allow the children to share their pictures and sentences. Make a class book with the illustrated sentences.

---

# Two-Day Format:

**Before:**
- Cover Talk (See Day 1, page 155.)
- Building Background Knowledge and Making Connections (See Day 1, page 155.)

**During:**
- Read Aloud (See Day 1, page 155.)
- Shared Reading (See Day 1, page 155.)

**After:**
- Introducing Nonfiction Elements (See Day 2, page 155.)

**Before:**
- Picture Walk (See Day 1, page 155.)

**During:**
- Choral Reading (See Day 4, page 156.)

**After:**
- Summarizing (See Day 3, page 156.)
- Writing and Drawing (See Day 5, above.)

**Predictable Chart Idea:**
_____ come(s) from _____.
<u>Carrots</u> come from <u>my garden</u>. (Mrs. Mitchell)
<u>Ice cream</u> comes from <u>milk</u>. (Jeff)
<u>Bread</u> comes from <u>the bakery</u>. (Chris)

**Theme:**
This may be an appropriate time to do a nutrition or farm products theme.

---

# Who's in the Shed?

## by Brenda Parkes
### (Rigby, 1986)

A group of farmyard animals wakes up to howling, growling, roaring, and clawing. They notice something being placed in the shed. The curious animals all have the same question, "Who's in the shed?" One at a time, they all get a peek. Finally, the creature in the shed is revealed. It is a bear, and he does not like animals that stare. Children will also want to peek through the holes and windows along with the animals to find out, "Who's in the shed?"

**Purpose:**
Build background knowledge and read for enjoyment.
**Preparation/Materials Needed:**
• Drawing paper and crayons

**Before:**
• Cover Talk—Ask, "What do you notice? What is the dog doing?"
• Previewing—Read only the first three pages of the text.
• Building Background Knowledge and Making Connections—Ask, "Who do you think is in the shed?" Write the students' responses on the board, transparency, or chart paper).

**During:**
• Read Aloud—Read the big book aloud to the students with full expression.
• Shared Reading—Invite the students to join in and share the reading.

**After:**
• Writing and Drawing—Have the students copy and complete the following sentence: A _____ is in the shed. Allow students to illustrate their papers and share them with the class.

---

**Purpose:**
Identify the beginning, the middle, and the end of the story.
**Preparation/Materials Needed:**
• Beach Ball with questions
• Three sentence strips
• Index cards
• Pocket chart
• Write the following headings on the index cards: **Beginning, Middle, End**. Place the headings cards in the pocket chart

**Before:**
• Retelling—Allow children to retell the story during a picture walk.

**During:**
• Echo Reading—Read a line and let the children be your echo, repeating the line after you.

**After:**
• Discussion and Writing—Ask, "What happened at the beginning? In the middle? At the end?" Write the responses on sentence strips and place them under the correct headings in the pocket chart.
• Beach Ball Questions—Toss the beach ball. Assist the student who catches the ball in reading one of the questions. Allow students to answer the question. Encourage them to refer to the pocket chart or book cover when giving their answers.

**Purpose:**
Highlight the animal sounds.
**Preparation/Materials Needed:**
- Highlighting tape

**Before:**
- Retelling—Use the cover as a catalyst for retelling the story.

**During:**
- Echo Reading—Read a line and let the children be your echo, repeating the line after you.
- Choral Reading and Highlighting—Stop after each two-page spread. Allow students to find and highlight the animal sounds. Make sure to talk with the students about how they located the sound words.

**After:**
- Discussion—Talk about what students thought was in the shed and what was really in the shed.

---

**Purpose:**
Round Up the Rhymes and use spelling patterns to read some new words.
**Preparation/Materials Needed:**
- Chart paper or transparency
- Highlighting tape
- Highlight the following words in the big book: **sheep**, **peep**, **then**, **hen**, **big**, **pig**.

**Before:**
- Reviewing—Talk about the story and rhyming words. Have the children listen for rhyming words as they read the story again.

**During:**
- Choral Reading—The whole class reads the text with you or you can assign parts to be read by different children. Ask, "What did you notice today as we read the story? Which words were highlighted?"

**After:**
- Finding and Writing—Find the highlighted words. Write the rhyming pairs on the chart paper or transparency. If needed, direct children to observe that there are pairs of words that rhyme and have the same spelling pattern.
- Transfer Words—Have the children underline the spelling pattern in the rhyming words. Write two words under each underlined pattern and see if students can read them. Ask, "What if I was reading and came to this word (**deep**, **creep**; **pen**, **when**; **dig**, **twig**)?"

---

**Purpose:**
Participate in Doing the Book.
**Preparation/Materials Needed:**
- The "Props"—pictures of a **sheep**, a **cow**, a **horse**, a **hen**, a **pig**, and a **bear**.

**Before:**
- Presenting the Props—Discuss how to use the props in Doing the Book.
- Picture Walk—Confirm the actions and their sequence for Doing the Book.

**During:**
- Doing the Book—Pass out the props. The class choral reads the text while the characters pantomime the actions. Repeat, allowing every child to participate in the pantomime.

**After:**
- Discussion—Talk about the story. Ask, "Did this really happen? Could it really happen?"

---

## Two-Day Format:

**Before:**
  • Cover Talk (See Day 1, page 158.)
**During:**
  • Read Aloud (See Day 1, page 158.)
  • Shared Reading (See Day 1, page 158.)
**After:**
  • Discussion and Writing (See Day 2, page 158.)

**Before:**
  • Picture Walk (See Day 1, page 158.)
**During:**
  • Choral Reading and Highlighting (See Day 3, page 159.)
**After:**
  • Doing the Book (See Day 5, page 159.)

# EXTENSIONS

### Theme
This would be an appropriate book to use for an animal or fair theme.

### Predictable Chart Idea:
A _____ is in the shed.
A <u>cat</u> is in the shed. (Mrs. Hall)
A <u>dog</u> is in the shed. (Barbara)
A <u>mouse</u> is in the shed. (Jorge)
A <u>squirrel</u> is in the shed. (Ashley)

### Interactive Chart:
I thought a wolf was in the shed.
I thought a tiger was in the shed.
I thought a monster was in the shed
But it was a circus bear!

---

# Shared Reading
# with
# Big Books

## Additional Extensions

## Chickens
### pages 35-37

**Science:**
Incubate an egg. Keep a daily journal of observations.

**Internet Resource:**
Facts about chickens:
http://www.enchantedlearning.com/subjects/birds/printouts/Chickenprintout.shtml

## Dinosaurs, Dinosaurs
### pages 41-43

**Read-Aloud Books:**
- *If the Dinosaurs Came Back* by Bernard Most (Harcourt, 1978)
- *Danny and the Dinosaur* by Syd Hoff (HarperCollins Juvenile Books, 1993)
- *A Dinosaur Named after Me* by Bernard Most (Voyager Books, 1995)

**Internet Resources:**
- http://www.bernardmost.com
- http://www.enchantedlearning.com/subjects/dinosaurs/index.html

## The Farm Concert
### pages 50-52

**Internet Resource:**
*What Do I Say?*—a reproducible book about animals and their sounds
http://www.enchantedlearning.com/whatdoisay/

# Feathers for Lunch
## pages 53-55

**Read-Aloud Books:**
- *Cats* by Gail Gibbons (Holiday House, Inc., 1998)
- *Why Do Cats Meow?* by Joan Holub (Puffin, 2001)
- *Have You Seen Birds?* by Joanne F. Oppenheim (Scholastic, Inc., 1990)
- *Birdsong* by Audrey Wood (Harcourt Brace, 1997)
- *Top Cat* by Lois Ehlert (Harcourt Brace, 1998)
- *Have You Seen My Cat?* by Eric Carle (Aladdin Books, 1997)
- *Millions of Cats* by Wanda Gag (Paper Star, 1996)

**Science:**
Place a bird feeder outside a classroom window. Observe and write down the names of the birds that come to feed.

**Internet Resources:**
Facts about birds:

http://www.enchantedlearning.com/subjects/birds/Allaboutbirds.html
http://www.enchantedlearning.com/subjects/birds/Birdextremes.shtml

Pictures to color:

http://www.enchantedlearning.com/subjects/birds/printouts/

# Growing Vegetable Soup
## pages 62-64

**Label:**
Use self-stick notes to clearly label the vegetables and tools pictured in the book.

**Science:**
Grow some of the plants needed for vegetable soup. Observe and write the growth process.

# I Love Spiders
## pages 68-70

**Read-Aloud Book:**
- *The Itsy Bitsy Spider* by Iza Trapani (Charlesbridge Publishing, 1998)

**Souvenir:**
Make a spider using construction paper and/or chenille craft sticks.

# In a Dark, Dark Wood
## pages 77-79

**Interactive Chart Idea:**
Use the text pattern in this story to write a new story, *In a Dark, Dark School*.

> In a dark, dark school, there was a creepy, creepy hall.
> In the creepy, creepy hall, there was a spooky, spooky classroom.

# In the Tall, Tall, Grass
## pages 80-82

**Science:**
Explore the natural habitats near your school. Make sure to bring along some magnifying glasses. Clipboards would also be helpful and enable children to take notes and illustrate what they see.

**Read-Aloud Book:**
• *In the Small, Small Pond* by Denise Fleming (Henry Holt and Co., Inc., 1998)

# It Begins with an A
## pages 83-85

**Tongue Twisters:**
Create initial consonant tongue twisters. For example: Joe and Jennifer jump and jiggle. *An Alphabet Book of Cats and Dogs* by Shelia Moxley (Little Brown, 2001) provides excellent examples for creating these tongue twisters.

**Riddles:**
Create new riddles for other words. For example: It is my favorite pet. It begins with D. It is always at my door to say hi to me! (dog)

# It Looked Like Spilt Milk
## pages 86-88

**Predictable Chart Ideas:**
It looked like a _____, but it wasn't.
It looked like a <u>cupcake</u>, but it wasn't. (Mrs. Peachtree)
It looked like an <u>elephant</u>, but it wasn't. (Duane)
It looked like an <u>earring</u>, but it wasn't (Jimmy Lee)
Note: Create cotton ball clouds for the illustrations of these sentences.

**Science:**
Write and graph cloud-cover data and other weather-related information on a daily basis while reading this book.

**Label:**
Use self-stick notes to label all of the objects in the story.

# Jeb's Barn
## pages 89-91

**Predictable Chart Ideas:**
I would like to build a _____.
I would like to build a skyscraper. (Mr. Carpenter)
I would like to build a race car. (Leon)
I would like to build a dollhouse. (Ida)

**Career Study:**
Construction jobs

**Field Trip:**
Visit a home construction site.

**Center Activity:**
Allow children to build houses with building blocks or other building toys.

# Meanies
## pages 107-109

**Predictable Chart Ideas:**
A Meanie likes to _____.
A Meanie likes to go to the dump. (Mrs. Colorman)
A Meanie likes to sleep in the bathtub. (Jerrica)
A Meanie likes to chew old tires. (Anthony)

The boys and girls like to _____.
The boys and girls like to read books. (Mrs. Friendly)
The boys and girls like to talk a lot. (Deonte)
The boys and girls like to eat pizza. (Franchesca)

# Monster Sandwich
## pages 110-112

**Read-Aloud Books:**
- *Peanut Butter and Jelly: A Play Rhyme* by Nadine Bernard Westcott (E. P. Dutton, 1992)
- *Sandwiches, Sandwiches* by Jeffery Stoodt (Steck-Vaughn, 1997) Available only in six-packs.
- *Lunch* by Denise Fleming (Henry Holt and Co., Inc., 1998)

**Theme:**
This may be an appropriate time to do a nutrition theme.

# The Napping House
## pages 119-121

**Interactive Chart Idea:**

"Roll Over"

In addition to changing the number words, change one or both of the groups of boxed words.

There were **five** in a bed.
And the little one said, "Roll Over! Roll Over!"
So they all rolled over
And one fell out.

There were **four** in a bed.
And the little one said, "I'm Cold! I'm Cold!"
So they all covered up
And one fell out.

There were **three** in a bed,
And the little one said, "Stop pushing! Stop pushing!"
So they all pushed some more
And one fell out.

# Shoes from Grandpa
## pages 140-142

**Read-Aloud Books:**
- *New Shoes for Sylvia* by Joanna Hurwitz (William Morrow and Co., 1999)
- *Red Dancing Shoes* by Denise Lewis Patrick (William Morrow and Co., 1998)
- *Shoes* by Elizabeth Winthrop (HarperCollins Children's Books, 1988)

# Splish, Splash
## pages 146-148

**Read-Aloud Books:**
- *Polar Bear, Polar Bear, What Do You Hear?* by Bill Martin, Jr. (Henry Holt and Co., Inc., 1991)
- *Cock-A-Doodle-Moo!* by Bernard Most (Harcourt, 1996)
- *Barnyard Banter* by Elizabeth Winthrop (Henry Holt and Co., Inc., 1994)

# Today Is Monday
## pages 152-154

**Interactive Chart Ideas:**
Games, colors, etc., can be used to replace food. For example: Friday, kickball; Saturday, football; Sunday, jump rope.

**Read-Aloud Books:**
- *All through the Week with Cat and Dog* by Rozanne L. Williams (Creative Teaching Press, 1995)
- *The Very Hungry Caterpillar* by Eric Carle (Putnam Publishing Group, 1984)

# Where Does Breakfast Come From?
## pages 155-157

**Read-Aloud Books:**
- *Green Eggs and Ham* by Dr. Seuss (Random House, 1976)
- *What's on My Plate?* by Ruth Belov Gross (Atheneum, 1990)
- *Milk, From Cow to Carton* by Aliki (HarperCollins Juvenile Books, 1992)
- *The Milk Makers* by Gail Gibbons (Aladdin Paperbacks, 1987)
- *Bread, Bread, Bread* by Ann Morris (HarperCollins Children's Books, 1993)

_____
mouse

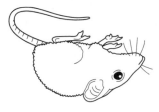

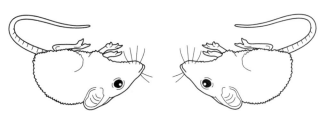

yellow mouse + blue mouse

_____
mouse

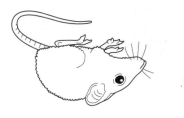

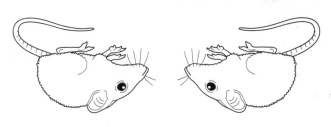

red mouse + blue mouse

yellow mouse + red mouse

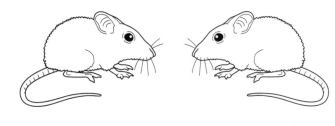

_____ mouse

Yellow and red make orange.

## Mouse Colors

blue mouse     red mouse

yellow mouse

# Shared Reading with Big Books

**References**

## Professional References

Cunningham, P. M. and Hall, D. P. (2000) *True Stories from Four-Blocks® Classrooms*. Greensboro, NC: Carson-Dellosa.

Cunningham, P. M., Hall, D. P., and Cunningham, J. W. (2000) *Guided Reading the Four-Blocks® Way*. Greensboro, NC: Carson-Dellosa Publishing Co.

Cunningham, P. M., Hall, D. P., and Sigmon, C. M. (1998) *The Teacher's Guide to the Four Blocks®*. Greensboro, NC: Carson-Dellosa Publishing Co.

Hall, D. P. and Cunningham, P. M. (1997) *Month-by-Month Reading and Writing for Kindergarten*. Greensboro, NC: Carson-Dellosa Publishing Co.

Hall, D. P. and Williams, E. (2000) *The Teacher's Guide to Building Blocks™*. Greensboro, NC: Carson-Dellosa Publishing Co.

## Big Books Cited

Note: The ISBN or Product Number (PN) has been included to assist in purchasing. Please note that many of these big books are available only from a teacher-supply store or the publisher.

*A Pair of Socks* by Stuart J. Murphy (Scholastic Big Books, 1996) [ISBN 0-590-92109-3]

*Across the Stream* by Mirra Ginsburg (Scholastic Big Books, 1982) [ISBN 0-590-73305-2]

*Any Kind of Dog* by Lynn Heiser (Harcourt School, 1992) [ISBN 0-153-06878-7]

*As the Crow Flies: A First Book of Maps* by Gail Hartman (Macmillan/McGraw Hill, 1991) [ISBN 0-02-17905-1]

*Brown Bear, Brown Bear, What Do You See?* by Bill Martin, Jr. (Harcourt Brace School, 1993) [ISBN 0-153-00283-2]

*Building a House* by Byron Barton (Hampton Brown, 1992) [ISBN 1-563-34182-4]

*The Carrot Seed* by Ruth Krauss (Scholastic Big Books, 1945) [ISBN 0-590-73301-X]

*Carry-Out Food* by Andrea Butler (Rigby, 1987) [PN 06398C00]

*Chickens* by Diane Snowball (Mondo, 1995) [PN 50473]

*Cookie's Week* by Cindy Ward (Scholastic Big Books, 1988) [ISBN 0-590-72700-1]

*Dinosaurs, Dinosaurs* by Byron Barton (HarperCollins, 1991) [ISBN 0-060-20410-9]

*The Doorbell Rang* by Pat Hutchins (Scholastic Big Books, 1986) [ISBN 0-590-6511-9]

*The Enormous Watermelon* by Brenda Parkes and Judith Smith (Rigby, 1986) [ISBN 073120034]

*The Farm Concert* by Joy Cowley (Wright Group, 1998) [ISBN 0-780-27666-3]

*From Head to Toe* by Eric Carle (Harcourt School, 1997) [ISBN 0-153-13373-2]

*Feathers for Lunch* by Lois Ehlert (Harcourt Brace, 1993) [ISBN 0-152-30551-3]

*Freight Train* by Donald Crews (Mulberry Books, 1978) [ISBN 0-688-12940-4]

*Growing Vegetable Soup* by Lois Ehlert (Harcourt Brace, 1991) [ISBN 0-152-32581-6]

*I Like Me!* by Nancy Carlson (Scholastic Big Books, 1998) [ISBN 0-590-18367-2]

*I Love Spiders* by John Parker (Scholastic Big Books, 1988) [ISBN 0-590-65209-5]

*If the Dinosaurs Came Back* by Bernard Most (Harcourt Brace, 1978) [ISBN 0-152-38022-1]

*If You Give a Mouse a Cookie* by Laura Joffe Numeroff (HarperCollins Children's Books, 1996) [ISBN 0-064-43409-5]

*In a Dark, Dark Wood: A Traditional Tale* illustrated by Christine Ross (Wright Group, 1998) [ISBN 0-780-27659-0]

*In the Tall, Tall Grass* by Denise Fleming (Henry Holt, 1993) [ISBN 0-805-02950-8]

*It Begins with an A* by Stephanie Calmenson (Scholastic Big Books, 1993) [ISBN 0-590-72908-X]

*It Looked Like Spilt Milk* by Charles G. Shaw (HarperCollins, 1992) [ISBN 0-064-43312-9]

*Jeb's Barn* by Andrea Butler (Celebration Press, 1995) [0-673-76121-5]

*The Jigaree* by Joy Cowley (Wright Group, 1998) [ISBN 0-780-27667-1]

*Jump, Frog, Jump!* by Robert Kalan (Mulberry Books, 1995) [ISBN 0-688-14849-2]

*The Little Red Hen* retold by Brenda Parkes and Judith Smith (Rigby, 1984) [ISBN 0-454-00935-6]

*Lunch* by Denise Fleming (Harcourt Brace, 1992) [ISBN 0-153-06893-0]

*Mary Had a Little Lamb* by Sarah Josepha Hale (Scholastic Big Books, 1990) [ISBN 0-590-72755-9]

*Meanies* by Joy Cowley (Wright Group, 1998) [ISBN 0-780-27668-X]

*Monster Sandwich* by Joy Cowley (Wright Group, 1998) [ISBN 0-780-27628-0]

*Mouse Paint* by Ellen Stoll Walsh (Harcourt Brace, 1989) [ISBN 0-152-56026-2]

*Mud Walk* by Joy Cowley (Wright Group, 2000) [ISBN 0-322-02463-3]

*Oh No!* by Bronwen Scarffe (Mondo, 1994) [ISBN 1-57255-535-1]

*The Napping House* by Audrey Wood (Harcourt Brace, 1984) [ISBN 0-152-56711-9]

*Peanut Butter and Jelly: A Play Rhyme* by Nadine Bernard Westcott (Harcourt School, 1987) [0-153-13383-X]

*The Pig That Learned to Jig* by Alan Trussell Cullen (Wright Group, 1993) [ISBN 0-780-22827-8]

*The Popcorn Popper* by JoAnne Nelson (Modern Curriculum Press, 1992) [ISBN 0-813-61111-3]

*Pumpkin, Pumpkin* by Jeanne Tigherington (Scholastic Big Books, 1986) [ISBN 0-395-73154-2]

*Quick as a Cricket* by Audrey Wood (Childs Play, 1997) [ISBN 0-859-53331-X]

*Silly Sally* by Audrey Wood (Harcourt Brace, 1992) [ISBN 0-152-00072-0]

*Splish, Splash* by Jeff Sheppard (Harcourt School, 1994) [ISBN 0-153-06879-5]

*Three Little Kittens* by Paul Galdone (Houghton Mifflin, 1986) [ISBN 0-395-75252-3]

*Today Is Monday* by Eric Carle (Philomel Books, 1993) [ISBN 0-399-21966-8]

*Where Does Breakfast Come From?* by David Flint (Rigby, 1998) [PN 726983C00]

*Who's in the Shed?* by Brenda Parkes (Rigby, 1986) [ISBN 0-731-20029-2]

## Other Children's Books Cited

Note: Please note that many of these books are available only in certain formats and will need to be ordered from a teacher-supply store or the publisher.

*101 Cars on the Track* by Sam Wilson (Cartwheel Books, 2001)

*ABC I Like Me!* by Nancy Carlson (Puffin, 1997)

*All through the Week with Cat and Dog* by Rozanne L. Williams (Creative Teaching Press, 1995)

*An Alphabet Book of Cats and Dogs* by Shelia Moxley (Little, Brown and Co., 2001)

*Apples and Pumpkins* by Anne Rockwell (Simon and Schuster Children's, 1994)

*Arf! Beg! Catch! Dogs from A to Z* by Henry Horenstein (Scholastic, Inc., 1999)

*Barnyard Banter* by Denise Fleming (Henry Holt and Co., Inc., 1994)

*Beep Beep, Vroom Vroom!* by Stuart J. Murphy (HarperCollins Juvenile Books, 2000)

*Birdsong* by Audrey Wood (Harcourt Brace, 1997)

*Bob's Birthday* by Diane Redmond (Simon Spotlight, 2001)

*Bones, Bones, Dinosaur Bones* by Byron Barton (Ty Crowell Co., 1990)

*Bread, Bread, Bread* by Ann Morris (HarperCollins Children's Books, 1993)

*Building a House* by Annette Smith, Jenny Giles, and Beverley Randell (Rigby, 2001) Only available in six-packs.

*Building a House* by Byron Barton (William Morrow and Co., 1990)

*Caps For Sale* by Eshpyr Slobodkina (HarperTrophy, 1987)

*Cats* by Gail Gibbons (Holiday House, Inc., 1996)

*Chick: Watch Me Grow!* by Nancy Sheehan (Penguin, 2000)

*The Chicken or the Egg* by Allan Fowler (Children's Press, 1993)

*Clap Your Hands* by Lorinda Bryan Cauley (Paper Star, 1997)

*The Cloud Book* by Tomie de Paola (Holiday House, Inc., 1986)

*Clouds* by Roy Wandelmaier (Troll Communications, 1990)

*Cock-A-Doodle-Moo!* by Bernard Most (Harcourt, 1996)

*Color Farm* by Lois Ehlert (HarperCollins Children's Books, 1990)

*Color Zoo* by Lois Ehlert (HarperCollins Children's Books, 1999)

*Danny and the Dinosaur* by Syd Hoff (HarperCollins Juvenile Books, 1993)

*A Day at Greenhill Farm* by Sue Nicholson (DK Publishing, 1998)

*Days with Frog and Toad* by Arnold Lobel (HarperCollins, 1984)

*Digging Up Dinosaurs* by Aliki (HarperTrophy, 1988)

*Dinosaur Cousins?* by Bernard Most (Voyager Books, 1990)

*A Dinosaur Named after Me* by Bernard Most (Voyager Books, 1995)

*Dinosaur Time* by Peggy Parish (HarperCollins Children's Books, 1987)

*Divide and Ride* by Stuart J. Murphy (Scott Foresman, 1997)

*Dots, Spots, Speckles, and Stripes* by Tana Hoban (Greenwillow Books, 1987)

*Dr. Seuss's ABC* by Dr. Seuss (Random House, 1963)

*The Easter Egg Farm* by Mary Jane Auch (Holiday House, Inc., 1994)

*Eating the Alphabet* by Lois Ehlert (Harcourt Brace, 1989)

*Egg to Chick* by Millicent Ellis Selsom (HarperTrophy, 1987)

*The Enormous Watermelon* retold by Brenda Parkes and Judith Smith (Rigby, 1986) Only available in big book format or six-packs.

*The Farm Concert* by Joy Cowley (Wright Group, 1998) Only available in big book format or six-packs.

*The Farmer Didn't Wake Up* by Tamara Nunn (Creative Teaching Press, 1997) Only available in six-packs.

*Feathers for Lunch* by Lois Ehlert (Harcourt, 1990)

*Frog and Toad All Year* by Arnold Lobel (HarperCollins, 1984)

*Frog and Toad Are Friends* by Arnold Lobel (HarperCollins, 1979)

*Frogs* by Tom Williams (Wright Group) Only available in six-packs.

*Frog and Toad Together* by Arnold Lobel (HarperCollins, 1979)

*Glad Monster, Sad Monster: A Book about Feelings* by Ed Emberly and Susan Miranda (Little, Brown and Co., 1997)

*Green Eggs and Ham* by Dr. Seuss (Random House, 1976)

*Have You Seen Birds?* by Joanne F. Oppenheim (Scholastic, Inc., 1990)

*Have You Seen My Cat?* by Eric Carle (Aladdin, 1997)

*Hi, Clouds* by Carol Greene (Children's Press, 1983)

*Hop Jump* by Ellen Stoll Walsh (Voyager Books, 1996)

*Horton Hatches an Egg* by Dr. Seuss (Random House, 1976)

*Houses and Homes (Around the World Series)* by Ann Morris (Mulberry Books, 1995)

*How a House Is Built* by Gail Gibbons (Holiday House, Inc., 1996)

*How about a Hug?* by Nancy Carlson (Viking Children's Books, 2001)

*How Big Were the Dinosaurs?* by Bernard Most (Voyager Books, 1995)

*I Love Trains* by Philomen Sturges (HarperCollins Juvenile, 2001)

*If It Weren't for Farmers* by Allan Fowler (Children's Press, 1993)

*If the Dinosaurs Came Back* by Bernard Most (Voyager, 1978)

*If You Give a Moose a Muffin* by Laura Numeroff (Scott Foresman, 1991)

*If You Give a Pig a Pancake* by Laura Numeroff (HarperCollins Juvenile Books, 1998)

*If You Take a Mouse to the Movies* by Laura Numeroff (HarperCollins Juvenile Books, 2000)

*In a Dark, Dark Room and Other Scary Stories* by Alvin Schwartz (HarperCollins Juvenile Books, 1984)

*In a Scary Old House* by Harriet Ziefert (Penguin USA, 1989)

*In the Haunted House* by Eve Bunting (Clarion Books, 1990)

*In the Small, Small Pond* by Denise Fleming (Henry Holt and Co., Inc., 1998)

*It's Pumpkin Time* by Zoe Hall and Shari Halpern (Scholastic, Inc., 1999)

*The Itsy Bitsy Spider* by Iza Trapani (Charlesbridge Publishing, 1998)

*The Jigaree* by Joy Cowley (Wright Group, 2000) Only available in big book format or six-packs.

*The Jigaree's Breakfast* by Joy Cowley (Wright Group, 2000) Only available in big book format or six-packs.

*Life Is Fun* by Nancy Carlson (Puffin, 1996)

*Little Cloud* by Eric Carle (Putnam Publishing Group, 1996)

*The Little Engine that Could* by Watty Piper (Grosset and Dunlap, 1978)

*The Little Mouse, the Red Ripe Strawberry, and the Big Hungry Bear* by Audrey Wood (Child's Play, 1998)

*The Little Red Hen* by Byron Barton (HarperCollins Juvenile Books, 1994)

*The Little Red Hen* by Paul Galdone (Houghton Miffin, 1979)

*The Little Red Hen* by Lucinda McQueen (Scholastic Big Books, 1993)

*Little Red Hen (Makes a Pizza)* by Philemon Sturges (Dutton Books, 1999)

*Lunch* by Denise Fleming (Henry Holt and Co., Inc., 1998)

*Make Way for Ducklings* by Robert McCloskey (Viking Children's Books, 1976)

*Mapping Penny's World* by Loreen Leedy (Henry Holt Books for Young Readers, 2000)

*Me on the Map* by Joan Sweeney (Crown Publishing Group, 1998)

*The Meanies Came to School* by Joy Cowley (Wright Group)

*A Meanies Party* by Joy Cowley (Wright Group)

*The Meanies' Trick* by Joy Cowley (Wright Group)

*Mike Mulligan and His Steam Shovel* by Virginia Burton (Houghton Mifflin Co., 1976)

*The Milk Makers* by Gail Gibbons (Aladdin Paperbacks, 1987)

*Milk, From Cow to Carton* by Aliki (HarperCollins Juvenile Books, 1992)

*Millions of Cats* by Wanda Gag (Paper Star, 1996)

*The Musicians of Bremen* by Brenda Parkes and Judith Smith (Rigby, 1987) Only available in six-packs.

*New Shoes* for Sylvia by Johanna Hurwitz (William Morrow and Co., 1999)

*Old Macdonald Had a Farm* illustrated by Pam Adams (Child's Play, 1989)

*Our New House* by Annette Smith, Jenny Giles and Beverley Randell (Rigby, 2001) Only available in six-packs.

*Peanut Butter and Jelly: A Play Rhyme* by Nadine Bernard Westcott (E. P. Dutton, 1992)

*Peeping Beauty* by Mary Jane Auch (Holiday House, Inc., 1995)

*Polar Bear, Polar Bear, What Do You Hear?* by Bill Martin, Jr. (Henry Holt and Co., Inc., 1991)

*The Popcorn Book* by Tomie de Paola (Holiday House, Inc., 1988)

*Popcorn* by Alex Moran (Harcourt, 2000)

*Pumpkin Day, Pumpkin Night* by Anne Rockwell (Walker and Co., 1999)

*Q is for Duck: An Alphabet Guessing Game* by Mary Elting and Michael Folsom (Houghton Mifflin Co., 1980)

*The Real Hole* by Beverly Cleary (Econo-Clad Books, 1999)

*Red Dancing Shoes* by Denise Lewis Patrick (William Morrow and Co., 1993)

*Rosie's Walk* by Pat Hutchins (Simon and Schuster Children's, 1968)

*Sandwiches, Sandwiches* by Jeffery Stoodt (Steck-Vaughn, 1997) Only available in classroom packs or six-packs.

*Scary Party* by Sue Hendra (Candlewick Press, 1998)

*Scoop Saves the Day* by Diane Redmond (Simon Spotlight, 2001)

*Sheep in a Jeep* by Nancy Shaw (Houghton Mifflin Co., 1988)

*Shoes* by Elizabeth Winthorp (HarperCollins Children's Books, 1988)

*Spunky Monkeys* on Parade by Stuart J. Murphy (HarperTrophy, 1999)

*Stanley* by Syd Hoff (HarperTrophy, 1992)

*Stone Soup* by Marcia Brown (Scott Foresman, 1989)

*The Surprise Garden* by Zoe Hall (HarperCollins, 1998)

*Surprise Puppy* by Judith Walker-Hodge (DK Publishing, 1998)

*Tale of a Tadpole* by Karen Wallace (DK Publishing, 1998)

*Taxi: A Book of City Words* by Betsy and Giulio Maestro (Houghton Mifflin Co., 1989)

*Teddy Bear, Teddy Bear* illustrated by Michael Hague (William Morrow and Co., 1993)

*Today Is Monday* by Eric Carle (Philomel, 1993)

*Tomorrow's Alphabet* by George Shannon (Econo-Clad Books, 1999)

*Too Many Pumpkins* by Linda White (Holiday House, Inc., 1997)

*Top Cat* by Lois Ehlert (Harcourt Brace, 1998)

*Tops and Bottoms* by Janet Stevens (Harcourt Brace, 1995)

*Two Little Trains* by Margaret Wise Brown (HarperCollins Juvenile Books, 2001)

*Vegetable Garden* by Douglas Florian (Voyager Books, 1996)

*The Very Hungry Caterpillar* by Eric Carle (Putnam Publishing Group, 1984)

*We're Going on a Bear Hunt* by Michael Rosen (Simon and Schuster Children's, 1989)

*What Can Jigaree's Do?* by Joy Cowley (Wright Group, 1998) Only available in six-packs.

*What Do You See in a Cloud?* by Allan Fowler (Children's Press, 1996)

*What Would You Like?* by Joy Cowley (Wright Group, 1989) Only available in big book format or six-packs.

*What's on My Plate?* by Ruth Belov Gross (Atheneum, 1990)

*Whatever Happened to the Dinosaurs?* by Bernard Most (Voyager Books, 1987)

*Where Do I Live?* by Neil Chesanow (Barrons Educational Series, Inc., 1995)

*Where the Wild Things Are* by Maurice Sendak (HarperTrophy, 1988)

*Whose Eggs Are These?* by Brian and Jillina Cutting (Wright Group, 1988) Only available in six-packs.

*Why Do Cats Meow?* by Joan Holub (Puffin, 2001)

*Why Do Dogs Bark?* by Joan Holub (Penguin Putnam Books for Young Readers, 2001)

*The Wide-Mouthed Frog: A Pop-Up Book* by Keith Faulkner (Dial Books for Young Readers, 1996)

*Zoo-Looking* by Mem Fox (Mondo, 1996)

## Internet Resources

The following Internet sites provide general information about the Four-Blocks® and Building-Blocks™ Literacy Models:

*http://www.carsondellosa.com*

*http://www.wfu.edu/~cunningh/fourblocks*

*http://www.blocks4reading.com*

*http://www.readinglady.com*

## Other Resources

Guided Reading Beach Balls (CD-1050) Carson-Dellosa Publishing Co.